CONTROLLING

PEOPLE

How to Recognize,
Understand, and Deal
with People Who
Try to Contol You

Other Books by Patricia Evans

Teen Torment
The Verbally Abusive Relationship
Verbal Abuse Survivors Speak Out

CONTROLLING PEOPLE

How to Recognize, Understand,
and Deal with People Who
Try to Contol You

PATRICIA EVANS
Author of *The Verbally Abusive Relationship*

Adams Media
Avon, Massachusetts

Published by
Adams Media, a division of F+W Media, Inc.
57 Littlefield Street, Avon, MA 02322
www.adamsmedia.com

ISBN 10: 1-58062-569-X
ISBN 13: 978-1-58062-569-2

Printed in the United States of America

20 19 18 17 16 15

Library of Congress Cataloging-in-Publication Data
Evans, Patricia
Controlling people : how to recognize, understand, and deal
with people who try to control you / by Patricia Evans
p.   cm.
Includes bibliographical references (p.) and index.
ISBN 1-58062-569-X
1. Control (Psychology) 2. Manipulative behavior.
3. Anger. 4. Interpersonal relations. I. Title
BF632.5 .E92   2001
158.2--dc21   2001046303

This publication is designed to provide accurate and authoritative information
with regard to the subject matter covered. It is sold with the understanding that
the publisher is not engaged in rendering legal, accounting, or other professional advice. If legal advice or other expert assistance is required, the services
of a competent professional person should be sought.
    —From a *Declaration of Principles* jointly adopted by a Committee of the
American Bar Association and a Committee of Publishers and Associations

"Enter In" on page xi reprinted with permission
of Melissa McIntosh Brown.

This book is available at quantity discounts for bulk purchases.
For information, call 1-800-289-0963.

TABLE OF CONTENTS

PART III

PART IV

Acknowledgments

This book would have never come to fruition without the support and encouragement of many thousands of people who shared their pain, insights, and experiences with me in order that we might know more. Thank you all.

I am especially grateful to my editors—Jennifer Lantagne, whose graceful diligence greatly assisted me in refining the manuscript's rough edges, and Claire Gerus for seeing this book through to publication. Thanks to my publisher, Adams Media Corporation, Bob Adams and staff for your faith in me. Thanks also to my agent, Helen McGrath, always available and supportive.

Many thanks to my very good friend, Linda Catron, who offered a cheering section, the solitude of her Tahoe retreat, and the companionship of her beloved dog, Baby.

For their valuable suggestions I thank my friends, Adrianna, Christopher, Linda, Marilyn, Phyllis, Ross, Sharon, and Teresa. And especially I thank my family for their loving support.

Enter In

I want to leave you
to your own unhappiness,
fat lip, cantankerous,
canker sore rage.
I want to leave you
to your Archie Bunker ways,
your kingdom of complaint:
You didn't. You don't. You won't.
I want to leave you,

but I always enter in.

And when I look in the mirror,
someone has taken my place—
someone duller, stupider,
fatter with shiftless,
dead-pan eyes.

—Melissa McIntosh Brown

Introduction

"You don't know what you're talking about."

"You're too sensitive."

"If you leave me I'll tell the courts what a bad parent you are. I'll take the kids from you."

"No one else will ever want you."

These and similar phrases flow from the mouths of those who try to control people. Such instances of verbal abuse and threats are sometimes followed by acts of violence. The following story is an example of such behavior, and of a controlling relationship.

In the mid-nineties I received a letter from a woman describing her refusal to succumb to her husband's attempts to control her. The woman's letter described how her spouse, whose behavior often frightened her, had grabbed the book she was reading, torn it into pieces, and dumped all of it in the trash.

I was appalled to read this. A book, for heaven's sake! But, as I read further, I was touched by this woman's courage: "I went out to the trash and gathered up every piece, then I sat at the kitchen table and carefully glued every piece together."

Six years later I was signing books when a woman came forward from the line, handed me her book all glued and taped together and said, "This is the book I wrote you about."

If you have ever wondered why some people try to control others, or why one particular person tries to control you, or why someone tries to control a whole group of people, or even if you find yourself wanting to control others, this book is for you.

You are not alone in your desire to understand the problem of control. Thousands of people have asked me, "Why would anyone act 'like that'?" They describe the way they've been treated, and they wonder what compels one to try to control others. "Why don't most people who try to control others see that they're being oppressive? Are they under a spell or what?" they ask.

Many people have also asked why they can't seem to stop attempting to control others, even when these destructive behaviors are driving their loved ones away. They often say that something seems to "come over" them and things "go wrong." At times, they are so unaware of their behavior and its impact that they don't realize that anything has gone wrong until it's too late—a loved one has left or violence has erupted.

If some people don't recognize their own attempts to control others, could they actually be under a spell? Does a spell explain oppressive and controlling acts toward not only individuals but also groups and even countries? If there is such a spell, what is it? Is there some compelling force behind it?

This book is a quest to find answers to these questions. It will take us on a journey of exploration through a maze of senseless behaviors woven into our world. By the end of our journey we'll be in a new place with a new perspective on the problem of control. And the journey itself may very well be spell-breaking.

Part I

I n Part I we will examine the problem of control and how, even without intending to, some people may attempt to control us. We will begin to see how a "spell" seems to come over them and, for the first time, we'll understand just why some people indulge in oppressive behavior. We will explore the nature of the spell, and we will learn why people who attempt to control us often don't realize how destructive they are. We will also meet a Spellbreaker—a person capable of breaking the spell—and we will find out how any one of us can become, or may already be, a Spellbreaker.

Chapter I

Sense and Nonsense

---

*Ignorance does not
justify oppression. It
only makes it possible.*

H ave you ever been puzzled or disturbed by the behavior of a family member, friend, or coworker and found yourself wondering, "What's going on? Why is he acting like that?" Or, "She doesn't understand what I'm saying no matter how I say it." Or, "He tells me I'm being _____, but I'm not. *It doesn't make sense.*"

> *May stepped into the company conference room. Her mind was on a thousand details. She was distracted because she was handling one of several small crises common to a small new business.*
>
> *"Surprise!" her employees shouted.*
>
> *"Happy Birthday!" resounded through the room.*
>
> *"Oh, my gosh! I completely forgot it was my birthday!" May was surprised and thrilled.*
>
> *"Oh, May, you did not forget your birthday," said Dee.*
>
> *"Yes, I did," May replied.*
>
> *"Come on, you remembered. You knew we'd have a party for you," said Dee, insistently.*
>
> *"No, honestly," said May.*
>
> *"You knew we'd have cake and you were just waiting for it. We know you were," Dee said snidely.*
>
> *"Not at all," said May.*
>
> *"Oh, come on, out with it. You're just pretending like you're surprised," said Dee.*
>
> *"Let's not argue, let's have the party," someone said.*
>
> *While everyone's attention turned to the cake, May felt frustrated and uneasy.*

Why did things like this happen with Dee? It all seems so crazy, *May thought.* Why did Dee act like that?

May just didn't know. And it didn't seem like anyone else in the room did either.

No one wants to spend party time watching an argument, *she thought.* But, *she also thought,* it wasn't an argument.

She had felt assaulted and forced to defend herself. Everyone else felt uncomfortable. She was getting depressed on her birthday.

The whole incident reminded her of other similar ones. "Let it roll off your back," people said.

Forgetting one's birthday may seem strange, but the point is that Dee was *unable* to hear May, she was *unable* to understand what May was trying to tell her, and that is the behavior of a person who tries to control you.

What is going on? If you have pondered similar incidents in your own life, you have already seen some important pieces of this puzzle. Not only have you brought them into view, but also you've properly identified them as "nonsensical." These incidents don't make sense to most people.

In a certain way, the person you encountered *couldn't* hear you, understand you, or know you, no matter how long he or she had known you, and no matter what you told them about yourself. The person who has defined your experience seems to have failed to grasp that you are a person with your own reality.

When people encounter controlling behavior, they often feel "erased," as if, to the perpetrator, they don't exist. In relationships, particularly, this kind of behavior sets the stage for all kinds of abuse. Trying to maintain this kind of relationship leaves one exhausted and subject to intense mental anguish and emotional pain, not to mention the possibility of physical battering.

Not hearing, understanding, or wanting to understand the "other" is behavior central not only to many of our everyday problems, but also to the violence that affects people's lives in every part of the world, every second of every day. Acts against others—whether cold and subtle, such as a contemptuous glance, or hot and explosive, such as a burst of rage—are, paradoxically, both senseless and understandable. And they are also attempts to control.

I invite you to unravel the mystery with me, to make sense out of the nonsense, to discover just what is going on. I think the reason we haven't yet found out just why people try to control others is because senselessness has become so familiar that it seems to be "just the way it is."

This book presents a specific view that, like a lens, sorts out our experiences so that they can be seen clearly, so that everything can be taken into account. I will make this lens as clear as possible, having faith that others will polish it with new insights and new applications.

As we look through the lens, we will see that those who are most harmful to us, even dangerous to us, feel a *need* to exert control over us. But recognizing oppressive behavior does not in itself solve the problem. To be effective we must ask and answer the question, "From whence does this need come?"

We will find that, even though childhood upbringing, cultural mores, economic injustices, and erroneous beliefs can all be major influences in perpetuating oppressive and controlling behaviors, they don't fully explain them. Something else does. But what? The answer is hidden in the shadows of ignorance and it is in many ways astonishing. The need to control is driven by a force so compelling that it is almost as if we are under its spell.

Difficulties revolve around our nonrecognition of this compelling force, a current so deep, so constant, and so unchanging that it is tantamount to evolution itself. It has had a continually increasing impact upon humanity, begging to be recognized, but it has not yet been attended to—indeed, it has only begun to be noticed. When we remain unaware of it, our people-problems gain momentum.

To understand this compelling force, we will explore its influence in our daily lives. Once we see its effects, we will know what it is and whether we can align with it rather than ignore or oppose it. *If we are aligned with the force, life gets better. If we oppose it, life in general becomes more chaotic.*

I invite you to join me in this journey of exploration. But be forewarned. We will meet some strange paradoxes along the way. Our journey will forge a path through a maze of illusory actions woven into our world. If you do join me, I am confident that we will not only come to know the compelling force behind oppressive and controlling behaviors but also come to understand how this very same force, *if recognized and understood, compels just the opposite—behaviors that support our individual lives on planet Earth.*

Finally, after identifying the compelling force and its effects—both negative and potentially positive—we will see how best to align with it in order to avoid the negative consequences of moving against it.

Are you ready to take this step? It means that we will cross a threshold together, taking what we discover through time well into the third millennium.

Chapter II

The Problem

A difficult problem is a master teacher. If you miss one tiny part of the solution early on, it can call you to task at any moment.

—"Nan"

Thousands of people have shared with me the intimate details of their attempts to free themselves from the influence of people who tried to control them. Others have shared their attempts to stop exerting controlling tactics against others. In those instances in which the "Controllers" became truly conscious of their behavior, they were shocked at what they discovered about themselves. They were horrified.

The wise words at the beginning of this chapter were spoken by a woman I'll call "Nan," a happily married career professional, a mother, and a grandmother. But Nan didn't always have happiness. At one time her life was in chaos. During that time she spent many courageous years trying to understand "what was wrong."

While she was growing up, the people who were responsible for her had acted senselessly against her—people who were old enough to know better—people who thought that they *were* sensible.

They had disparaged her, ridiculed her, and thus defined her. They had oppressed her and attempted to control her. The people who treated her this way were, in fact, her parents. They called her their "little numskull." They ignored her complaints with accusations: "Don't you talk back to me," "You think you're better than the rest of us." Most of the time, Nan felt sad, inadequate, and confused, but she wasn't sure why.

At nineteen, she met a charming and intelligent man, but upon marrying him, he changed drastically. In fact, instead of charming her as he had when courting her, he put her down, called her vile names, and yelled at her so much that she became traumatized and sick. She felt that if she stayed she would die from pain, but she didn't know what to do, because she was accused of causing it all. She didn't see herself as wise, nor did she know where to look for a solution. This, of course, made her task, to make sense of nonsense, extraordinarily difficult.

In time, she found some answers. She saw the nonsense for what it was. She had been surrounded by people who acted senselessly and who had attempted to control her. Her realization enabled her to leave her abuser and her past behind her, and to create order out of the chaos. Still she was perplexed. *Why* had senselessness run rampant through her life?

Families fall apart, people fight depression, or escape emotional pain with drugs. Whole industries are built around raising self-esteem and developing positive thinking. Therapies are developed to help us to gain a positive self-concept and products are sold to lighten our moods. But the problem itself—people trying to control people—is not solved.

The senselessness that ran rampant through Nan's life creates chaos in the lives of millions of people. This chaos calls us to task. It is like the clamor of an insatiable beast almost at our doorstep. What is it all about? What compels it? What are we supposed to learn? Do we have a clear perspective?

In personal relationships, many people have experienced inexplicable acts against them that are covert or overt attempts to control them. But even when they recognize this behavior for what it is, they thirst to understand. *Why would someone want to control me? Why can't he or she see that their behavior is destroying our relationship? Do they know what they're doing?*

A medical doctor told me the following:

> *My father isn't well. He's in his eighties, has a number of complications, and a bad prognosis. So with my sisters, their families, and my children, we all went to see him.*
>
> *While we were gathered at his bedside, he reminisced about his childhood and how terrible it was for him. He shuddered at the memory of criticism and angry outbursts. As he talked we learned that his own*

father had been really great with people and well liked by friends but, paradoxically, cruel at home. He took my breath away—that he could tell that story and not know that he treats us exactly the same way. It was incomprehensible. No matter how we have tried to tell him, he just doesn't get it! It makes no sense!

The doctor's father seemed so unaware. His behavior seemed to make no sense. Thinking of the world and the problems in it, I realized that many people have said almost the same thing.

Is it human fate that we should live in a world where people are as unaware as the doctor's father was? Is it preordained— as if some people, in keeping with a god's joke, were born to build "bad karma," while others were born to suffer its effects?

Since we've arrived without directions, albeit holy books abound, we make our map as we go. "Don't take that route," one person warns another. "Look what happened to me."

At the same time we see that some people, even those committed to treating others as they would be treated, paradoxically do just the *opposite*. Who can forget the sad epic of the nineties, a man who battered his wife, cursed and humiliated her in public, saying, "I treat people the way I want to be treated."

People who have indulged in controlling behaviors are often stunned when they realize what they've done. I have heard many people, from many different parts of the country, all say the same thing: "I am a horrible person." Some, literally unable to stomach the knowledge of their own behaviors, threw up. But even these found it exceedingly difficult to change, no matter how much they wanted to.

Of course none was a "horrible person." They simply felt horrible. Unlike the doctor's father, they had awakened. Prior to this awakening they had been oblivious to their own behavior and to its effects. *What compelling force has gripped them and seems even to have gripped the world?*

I don't believe that destruction and violence are the outcome of bad karma, joking gods, or jealous ones. Nor are they just human nature. I *do* believe that there is a perspective that we haven't yet seen, one that makes sense of oppressive behaviors designed to control others and explains why, in a great many cases, people are blind to the havoc they wreak. This book presents this unique perspective. It reveals just what compels people to control others, and why people who attempt to control others act as if they are under a spell.

In talking with people caught up in oppressive behaviors in everyday situations, I've found that while often their anguish and guilt were notable, their frustration and confusion over giving up their wayward ways were even more striking. A client sent me the following description of how he tried to control his partner by sometimes acting as if she didn't exist and at other times acting as if her very being was wrong:

> *No one witnessed it because I was nice and kind to our friends. But when no one was around I got very irrational and angry. Knowing how I acted, that I sounded crazy. I wanted to understand myself. I was always willing to get help for any problem in our relationship, but I never knew what the problem was. I feel terrible that I did these things. This is what I recall at the moment though I'm sure there were lots more.*
>
> *I gave her the silent treatment and left her to feel alone and isolated.*
>
> *I would act cold and aloof and then, when she asked what was wrong, I would act very cold and say, "There's nothing wrong."*
>
> *Sometimes I'd just drive off and not tell her when*

she looked forward to an evening at home.
I cut down her friends.
If she asked me a question I'd get angry.
I started telling her she was abnormal.
I told her I was a lot better off before I married her.
I told her she didn't know what she was doing.
When I realized what I'd done, I cried a lot. I want
to understand.

I recall another man's anguished plea. He had recently realized that he was hurting the people he wanted to love. "Why can't I take it ten minutes down the road? I just don't understand why I don't, when I'm determined that I will." "It" was his supportive and equitable treatment of his employees, and "ten minutes down the road" was his wife and family. In other words, he treated people rationally and respectfully at work, and couldn't understand why he couldn't do the same at home. He'd "seen" himself some time before we talked. He'd struggled with what he'd seen yet felt nothing but frustration, confusion, and desperation. His intentions to be supportive and equitable at home, while laudable, just didn't seem to be enough. During his commute from work he'd lecture himself. He'd be appreciative, polite, or at least businesslike, he told himself. But he wasn't.

Why wasn't he?

I have heard many similar stories and each was, to me, a newly found puzzle piece. Some stories brought a number of pieces together. Some gave tiny glimpses of the whole at a distance, some enhanced the tone and color, and others revealed mysteries like a child's picture-puzzle reveals objects hidden in the foliage.

The picture is now complete. The smallest pieces fit. Nothing, I hope, is overlooked. I present this picture to you with the belief that it will be both clear and revealing. It needs to be because it is a map of the problem.

If we can describe and name the problem, I believe that we will then see its solution. If the picture is very clear, the solution will be most evident. For instance, if the "problem" were a knot in a tangled cord and you could see and describe it clearly, "The cord goes up here, around here, down there, is looped back and across this," you would see the solution to the problem. You would know how to untie it. Similarly, we will explore this problem so that the solution is clear. The problem concerns why people act against people, oppressing them in attempts to control them.

It is important that we look directly at the problem and that we not get sidetracked. Some people, taking their cue from the perpetrators of oppressive behaviors, look in the *opposite* direction from where the problem lies. Influenced by the perpetrators, these people, in a backwards way, explain violence and abuse as caused by the victim—something a person was "asking for" or "at least partially responsible for," or "should have seen coming," or "created," or "deserved," or "wanted." Or they explain oppression as being the work of something bodiless, something beyond the world, beyond time and space altogether, something done by the personification of evil itself. The devil. Badness itself made it happen. But making up a "devil" to serve as a handy scapegoat would divert us from our search.

No doubt, most of us have at some time been mistreated by others or have unwittingly mistreated someone else. Apologies and forgiveness acknowledge our human failings. But some people who mistreat us declare that they've done nothing wrong, or were driven to it (by us), or had good intentions, so we've nothing to complain about. These people just don't view the wrongs that they do as *wrong*. Even the perpetrators of the most extreme acts against others often do not feel that they've done anything wrong.

For instance, the media reported that a letter prosecutors said was written by Timothy McVeigh, dated February 10, 1995, stated "I might as well do some good when I can be 100 [percent] effective." McVeigh was found guilty of the Oklahoma City bombing, an attack that shocked the world. It took place April 19, 1995, just a little more than two months after he'd written the letter.

The bombing was described as the bloodiest terrorist attack to take place on American soil. One hundred and sixty-eight people were killed and another 500 were wounded. To do some good?

An even deadlier terrorist attack was launched against America and freedom itself on September 11, 2001. The hijacked-plane bombings of the World Trade Center and the Pentagon stunned the world and cost more than 6,000 lives. Scholars tell us that the terrorists were "religious" extremists who believed that their horrifying acts against the innocent were mandated by God.

This terrorizing unconsciousness is what we call evil. However, a strikingly similar unconsciousness is evident in even very common and less pervasively destructive acts, such as striking a child to "get it to stop crying." Such acts against children destroy their ability to release their emotions, confuse them, and leave them with buried rage. I frequently hear that this kind of child battering, even toward babies as young as six months, is still going on.

While I am not in any way equating hitting a child with the quite different act of terrorism, I am pointing to the fact that they both arise from a terrifying unawareness on the part of the aggressor. And that in most cases, when people act against other people, they feel justified. They feel sensible.

If an act against a person is justified in the mind of the

perpetrator, it is, in a *backwards* way, said to be caused by the victim rather than by the perpetrator. Just the *opposite* of the truth.

A second fact is that wrongful acts, acts *against* people, usually bring about just the opposite of what the perpetrators intend. Going back to our previous examples: in one case, "to do some good," McVeigh does harm, and in the other, "to stop a child's crying," a person exacerbates the anguish that brought forth the child's crying in the first place.

If you have ever encountered a person who acted against you by harassing you, defining you, discriminating against you, or physically assaulting you, you may have noticed that the act was perpetrated against you as if you were deserving of it.

Whether they are experienced as horrifying, hurtful, or simply nonsensical, acts against others have certain commonalities. Primarily, they are as follows:

1. Perpetrators usually believe that their oppressive actions are necessary, even right. Their behavior is actually the opposite: unnecessary and wrong.
2. Generally, acts against others, that is, attempts to control others, eventually bring the perpetrators just the opposite of what they want.
3. Acts against others originate with a distortion or lack of awareness. Perpetrators almost universally believe that they see clearly and are aware: the *opposite* of reality.

When it comes to acts against others, of *what* are people unaware? I believe that this is a very important question, because if we can answer it, if we know *what* they are unaware of, we will have begun to unravel a knotty problem and to answer the question "Why do a great many people try to control other people?"

I'll never forget a case I encountered some years ago. A man became so difficult to live with that his wife separated from him, moving into an apartment a couple of blocks from their home. This she did after tolerating his growing misbehavior for more than twenty years. She had always held the hope that he would change, become gentle, kind, and loving, and that somehow the investment of her time and energy in all those years would be realized in a close relationship.

Her husband always wanted her back and even after two years hoped that she would return. With her encouragement he decided to talk with me. During our consultation, I asked him if he knew what his wife wanted—what change, if any, might bring her back?

He said, "She just wants me to be nice to her."

"Is it possible that you could be nice to her?" I asked.

"How can I be nice to her when I'm so angry that she left?"

As we talked, his approach to his problems became perfectly clear. Somehow he felt that if he were angry enough, frightening her with sudden outbursts and demonstrations of rage; yelled enough, showing her just how mad she made him; put her down and intimidated her enough, telling her she could never make it on her own; even hit her enough, she would pay attention and realize the error of her ways. She would come back. Clearly, his attempt to control her was what had driven her away in the first place. And he couldn't see it. *This* is what he was unaware of. That doesn't mean that he was crazy. I would say instead that he, like all perpetrators, had it *backwards*. People who act against others truly act in a backwards way, doing the opposite of what they would need to do to realize their goal.

In the previous example, both the wife and the husband wanted a close relationship, but closeness meant something completely different to each person. Each one's idea of closeness and how to achieve it was the opposite of the other's. One person's idea of how to achieve closeness was sure to fail and actually did. In fact, it ended all possibility of closeness.

As we continue exploring the maze of illusory actions woven into our world, we will find out why some people act against their own intentions, whether to achieve closeness or to "do some good." Since all oppressive acts have a backwards quality to them, they can be said to take place in the context of backwardness. We will find out just what it is that is actually backwards.

Even ordinary behaviors are inexplicable unless we are aware of the context in which they take place. Once we understand the context, we can begin to interpret the behaviors, and most important, to find out why the context of backwardness exists.

Let's first take a closer look at how important context is. If you saw me shouting and quickly looking around, my behavior would seem odd, certainly inexplicable. If you saw the context in which it took place—watching a basketball game—my actions would no longer be inexplicable. In this example, the context or broad view explains the specific: my behavior.

By knowing the context in which people act against others, we can begin to explain their acts.

Chapter III

Intentions

*Despite their good intentions
it turned out wrong.*

A s we have seen, acts against others take place in the context of backwardness. I believe that most people who act in oppressive ways, consciously or unconsciously, attempting to control others, are trying to meet a particular *need* that overrides their good intentions. Misdirected, they have sought to meet this need in extraordinarily destructive ways, *even while unaware of the need itself.* Ultimately, destructive behaviors never succeed in fulfilling the need. As a result, we are witness to cycles of destruction.

Since most people intend to "do right by others" and want to be treated the same way, why, in certain cases, do their good intentions and all their efforts to realize them, come to naught?

There is an old tale called "The Miller's Daughter." The miller gives away part of his property and all that is on it in a bargain with the devil. He gives away the property in exchange for riches, thinking that only an apple tree is lost. But, what the miller "thinks" isn't enough. He loses his daughter to the devil because *she* is there with the apple tree. He learns too late the sad news from his wife. The miller and his wife suffer tremendously from such a great loss. And the daughter, too, suffers severely, going through many trials before finally escaping from the devil to go on with her life.

What the miller knew or thought he knew was not enough. His good intentions just to gain wealth were not enough. He did not know that there was something that he did not know: that before he actually lost his daughter to the devil, he had lost her in another way. He had lost (if ever he'd had it) his ability to relate to her. If he truly related to his wife and daughter as real people with real lives of their own, he would have at least talked to them about giving away the field before he did it. He would have realized that since they were living on the property it was their backyard, too, and he would never have struck his ill-fated bargain. Or his daughter would have known his plan and would have stayed off the back property.

If only he'd asked. Instead the miller acted for everyone. Even with good intentions, everyone suffers if the ability to relate is lost. How could the miller have lost his ability to relate? Could the ancient tale still be relevant?

Do people even now speak and act for others? "We're going now." "You're not wearing that." "That's not what you want." "You knew. . ."

Just as I was writing about the miller, I had a miller experience myself. A kindly man arrived to repair some electronic equipment. I told him, "I'll be working in my office. If you have any questions, please just ask."

He was unable to hear that I was working and didn't ask about interrupting my work. Unconscious control shows up in just this way. Here is what happened.

Working on this manuscript, I was in the process of moving text via my computer software when my computer screen went blank. Everything was gone. Not even a bomb or a sad face appeared. In the deadly silence I rushed out to see what had happened. My first thought was "Did he electrocute himself?" He was fine. He was working.

He'd shut off the electricity to the whole building. If only he'd asked. But like the miller he acted without regard to me, as if he didn't know I was there. Had he been beside himself— somewhere else—when I told him I was working? Would he have heard me if I were someone else—a general, a supreme court judge?

I told the electrician about the miller. And he most graciously accepted the story. "I've learned an important lesson here today. I won't ever forget it. I didn't intend to spoil your book."

Unlike the man who destroyed his wife's book, tearing it into pieces, the electrician apologized and determined to change. He had no intention of interrupting my work. He just hadn't really seen me. People who do not really see or hear others, even when *intending* to help them, may do just the opposite.

An intention is like the rudder on a ship. It sets our course. Guides us toward our objectives. Describes our purpose. But even with the best of intentions, some people fail. And, even if they realize that they are off course, and so affirm their good intentions, "something happens" and they get the opposite of what they wanted. Why? If their intentions are *the best*, what goes wrong? Isn't a good intention, like the rudder on a ship, an ever-present guide? If it is, then how do things go wrong?

What can it be like for people who find they've failed to bring their intentions to fruition, like, for instance, the man who couldn't seem to follow through on his intention to "take it home to his family," or even the miller?

In order to see the dilemma some people are in, let us imagine the following episode.

We're each on a ship and the current has carried us along for a very long time. It has always done so. And we assume it will always take us where we need to go. But we're beginning to feel a bit uneasy. We sense that something is wrong just under the surface. Our ship has gone off course. Our world is not as safe and sane as we would like.

Our intention and the course we have come to expect does not hold. We've come under the influence of a new current. Some of us become aware of it and so we make the necessary adjustments. In a sense, we reset our rudder. But others, not realizing that they are off course, have compounded their error by holding firm, reaffirming their intention, only to get to where they don't want to go more quickly.

These people don't notice that they're moving more and more gradually off course. They don't notice until they see that the scenery is quite different from what they had expected. And even then, when they do notice something's wrong, they don't know why or what. No matter how firmly they have relied upon the rudder of good intentions, their good intentions are not manifested, because something else, quite unknown to them, has come into play and because it is a deep, strong, and hidden current, it is a very compelling force.

Chapter IV

Beside Yourself

---

*Where do people go when
they are beside themselves?*

A ttempts to control people bring about "people problems." Let us look now at the nature of a classic "people problem," one that shows us something important about people's attempts to control others.

In our everyday lives, most of us have observed kinds of behavior that under ordinary circumstances would be intolerable, but in extraordinary or overwhelming circumstances are both tolerated and understandable. The context in which the action takes place makes all the difference. For instance, in the extraordinary circumstance of a disaster, a person's behavior may change drastically. Someone experiencing a disaster may shout, swear, give orders, and in other ways assault, in a sense, whomever is around: "Get a tourniquet! Damn you! Hurry up!"

Knowing the circumstance explains the behavior. We even have words for this: "He was *beside himself* with fear," or in another circumstance, "She was *beside herself* with grief." Knowing when a person is momentarily beside themselves, we ignore the assaults and instead of shouting back or leaving, we cope gently with the situation.

Imagine witnessing or being told of a great personal disaster. If you experienced such a great shock, you might automatically grasp something nearby, a chair or table, for instance. Or you might stagger or in some other way show that you feel dislodged—beside yourself.

Disaster strikes suddenly, and when it does, our reality seems to collapse. We find ourselves adrift beyond time and space.

Commonly, people who are beside themselves try to take control of what's "out there" in any way they can. They've lost their inner connection, so they try to get a grip on something, anything—even someone.

When people are in this state, we not only say that they are beside themselves, we may also say that they don't know what they are doing. It is as if they are disconnected from their everyday reality. To reconnect, a person may not just get a grip on a table or chair to restore physical balance and contact, but may also try to get a grip, so to speak, in someone around them, wanting someone to be like the glove on their hand, an extension of themselves, instantly available to do their bidding.

People can be *beside themselves* for any number of reasons, including an overriding feeling of pain, urgency, or loss. When we know the context, we can make sense of the behavior. But how do we explain intolerable behavior in ordinary circumstances? What would similar behavior in an ordinary context tell us?

For example, Jack, on his way out the door one morning to purchase his favorite Sunday paper, sees the weather and shouts at Jill, "Get me my coat! Damn you! Hurry up!"

In this case, Jack isn't treating Jill as a person but as something else. His orders are loud and intimidating. They are attempts to control Jill. Does he know what he is doing? Isn't he acting as if he is *beside himself*, disconnected, just as if he had experienced a disaster and is trying to get a grip, metaphorically speaking, in someone around him? Doesn't he act as if he wants Jill to be an extension of himself, instantly available to do his bidding?

Yet he hasn't experienced a sudden disaster. If it wasn't a great shock that dislodged him from himself, then what was it? How has he become disconnected? And, if some disaster had dislodged him in the distant past, leaving him beside himself, what compels him to remain so, even now on an ordinary Sunday morning? Why, like the miller, can't he relate to his wife?

We will discover the answers in coming chapters. But first we will take a quick look at the "self" that a person is "beside" when people are "beside themselves."

Chapter V

The "Self" We Are Sometimes "Beside"

---

*Betrayal of the self is
a betrayal of nature.*

I f I ask you who you are and you describe yourself to me, you differentiate yourself from all that is not you: "I like this and not that. . . . This is how I do . . . This is how I feel. . . . This is what I think. . . ." and so on. As you define yourself, you articulate and affirm your inner reality, including your thoughts, views, opinions, feelings, motives, values, intentions, inclinations, abilities, talents, likes, dislikes, memories, and beliefs. In this way you exercise your personal freedom to define yourself.

Clearly, as time passes, the more experiences you have, the more people you meet, the more ideas you entertain, the more you will actually learn about yourself. For example, having tasted chocolate-walnut ice cream, you know if you prefer it to vanilla ice cream on any particular day at any particular time.

As you construct your personal reality through your experience of everyday life, you assimilate knowledge of yourself and of the world. Your experiences "come" to you through your sensations, feelings, and intuition and are organized by your mind in a meaningful way.

Your direct experience creates a picture of reality and of yourself in your mind. These images change, are revised and fine-tuned by exposure to the nuances of life. You can think about your experiences and you can think about yourself, your values, actions, ideals, goals, and so forth.

You can change your self-definition at any moment: "I used to be shy, but I'm not anymore." As you grow in self-awareness from childhood to adulthood, your self-definition will expand to include more than it did when you were a child. "At ten I was a pianist. Now, at age twenty, I'm not only a pianist, but also a composer."

Most of us build our identity in a gradual way, because we are open to experience, but some people describe a surprising and immediate "knowing" about some aspect of their inner nature.

An artist, for instance, might know that "this is what I want to do" when first introduced to fine art; a performer might know "this is home" when first on stage; A scholar might know "this is what I want to study," as world-renowned mythologist Joseph Campbell said when he was introduced to mythology as a child. This self-knowing is not available to a person who is beside him- or herself most of the time.

Becoming an individual is a process of creation, and each one of us participates in this process all of our lives. Becoming yourself is both a physical and a psychic process. "First I was a cell. Now I'm a person." "Once I couldn't read. Now I can write."

You can discover new talents and interests at any age. People who stay open to their inner inclinations and remain true to themselves commonly discover more about themselves throughout their life. After their physical growth is complete, their psychic expansion continues. Their awareness becomes ever deeper, broader, and more comprehensive, if they allow it.

In the process of defining yourself, you build your identity and at the same time you create an unseen parameter that includes all that is not physical about you. This unseen parameter is your psychic boundary.

Your Psychic Boundary

Without a psychic boundary, we would be like drops of ink diffused in a pool of water—easily absorbed into other people's definitions of us, even other people's purposes. We would come to believe that they are our own, without even realizing it.

Since your psychic boundary can't be seen, it can be helpful to think of it as a space or line between your inner spiritual, psychological world and the outer world—the culture in which you live and the people with whom you interact.

By giving a name (psychic boundary, for instance), to the unseen we can talk about aspects of ourselves that are not concrete. We do this when we speak of the ego, soul, spirit, or mind as if they were concrete, as if we could see them, though we really only see their manifestations.

As you read this book it may be useful to imagine your own unseen psychic boundary, because this is the boundary that is trespassed by anyone who attempts to control you.

Just as your physical boundary delineates your physical presence, your psychic boundary delineates all else that is you. It circumscribes that which is unseen about you—your individuality.

You are in charge of what passes through this boundary. When you take in or reject information (an event or experience) you act as the "gatekeeper." When you give or withhold consent—"I accept this" or "I don't accept that"—you open and close the gate.

Your cells protect you in a similar way, acting as the gatekeepers of your physical body, automatically taking in or rejecting various materials.

Interestingly, your physical boundary also has an unseen quality to it that seems to extend a little beyond you. The way this boundary is respected in different cultures is reflected in the varying distances people stand from one another. For example, if you and I were taking an otherwise empty elevator together and I did not know you, I would stand near one side of the elevator and, most likely, you would stand near the other.

If I were to stand right next to you, you would likely step back in protection of your physical boundary, feeling that I had attempted to trespass into your personal space, even if I hadn't touched you. If I bumped into you, I would apologize. But, if I were in the elevator with a two-year-old child in my care, I would not only stand next to her, I would even hold her hand. A child's boundaries are open to receive nurturing protection.

When we see the physical presence of a person, we see their individuality, stamped like a fingerprint in space/time. Physical boundaries are trespassed in acts of physical violation, for example, physical violence, sexual assault, and murder. Most of us have a pretty good idea of people's physical boundaries and manage to respect them. Those who don't are often arrested.

Clearly, just as assaults to the body are harmful, so are assaults to the psyche. All such assaults are attempts to control us. But we have only recently begun to recognize assaults against a person's psychic boundary—racial and gender slurs, and all categories of verbal abuse are examples. (See my earlier book, *The Verbally Abusive Relationship*: *How to Recognize It and How to Respond*, 1996, Adams Media Corporation, for an in-depth look at verbal abuse.)

Historically, we have given little thought to our psychic boundary. One reason is that we live in a world so *externally* focused that we became used to thinking, "what can't be seen, can't be." But with atom splitting, microwaves, newly discovered stars, and conversations in cyber-space, we realize that what can't be seen *can* be.

Since little attention is given to the reality of a psychic boundary, people may mix up their own reality with that of another person. This carries a great significance, because it allows all kinds of problems to develop in all kinds of relationships.

Your *self*, while having many invisible aspects, and many invisible qualities and characteristics, forms a whole. Each of us has a sense of this "whole," and it is this sense of self that we seem to lose, or to be dislodged from, when we suffer the trauma of a catastrophic event—even to the extent of amnesia, forgetting who we *are* and the context of our life.

Some events are so sudden that we don't quite take them

in, or we only manage to take them in slowly. Sudden events impact our psychic boundary, even shock us. If the jolt is more than we can handle, if we cannot close the gate on our experience, we may feel overwhelmed or "dislodged." If we are dislodged we then may be said to be beside ourselves.

I talked with an older friend about the experience people have of being beside themselves. My friend said that he had an old memory. He recalled being just two years old when his mother left him alone for a few hours with his older sister, and he recalled that at that exact time he realized that he felt secure and aware of himself. He said he had felt this sense of self most of the time ever since. Then he asked, "Is this the self that I would miss if I were beside myself?" I assured him that it was and marveled that he could have been so aware of himself at such an early age.

Thus far, we have seen that actions against people take place in the context of backwardness. The perpetrators seem to be beside themselves. When they attempt to control another person, acting against him or her, they assault either that person's psychic boundary, or physical boundary, or both. Or they ignore the other person as if he or she doesn't exist while taking control of his or her time, space, or other resources. We've seen, too, that a shock or crisis may leave people beside themselves and this has something to do with the problem of control. In the next chapter we will look at other ways people may become beside themselves.

Chapter VI

Disconnection: Training, Trying, and Trauma

It is our freedom
to define ourselves.

H ow can it be that some people appear to be beside themselves in the most ordinary circumstances? What could
lead a person to be beside himself when he hasn't been jolted
from himself by a shocking event? Are people who are beside
themselves more likely to fall under a spell? To understand how
Jack, in the earlier example, was beside himself when he shouted
at Jill to get his coat, we'll look in on one of Jack's early childhood experiences. Although this particular experience did not
cause Jack to be beside himself, it contributed to it. It would take
many such experiences and other influences for Jack to reach
the state he was in.

But, before we go on, please note two very significant
facts about Jack and anyone who attempts to control another
person: *People who act as if they are beside themselves in ordinary circumstances usually do so only in relation to certain
people.* For instance, they are not likely to ignore, define, put
down, order, yell at, or swear at their neighbors, their friends,
and the people they encounter in a casual way. Later in our
journey we'll see why. And, *when people are beside themselves,
they are essentially unaware of themselves.* We then might say
that they are disconnected.

Before we explore the ways disconnection takes place,
we'll stop for a moment to explore "the four functions,"
because people become disconnected when these functions
are impaired.

The Four Functions

Everyone is born with four functions: feeling, sensate, intuitive, and thinking. They allow us to be connected to ourselves.

These functions are the bases for a variety of tests used by
educators, employers, and career counselors to evaluate personality types, career goals, and learning styles.

Let's see how these functions work. When entering a room, one might notice the temperature and smells and colors (via the sensate function), while getting a sense of the mood of the people in the room (via the feeling function), while comparing the situation to a previous but similar gathering (via the thinking function), while having a sense that a friend who doesn't usually attend will be showing up any minute (via the intuitive function).

Although we come into the world fully equipped with these functions, if we stop using them, our ability to assimilate our experience and to understand ourselves and the world around us is impaired. If our ability to understand ourselves is not impaired, it is because our four functions give us the information we need to live and thrive. For instance, babies respond to their sensations. They know if they are wet, cold, hungry, or comfortable. They see, hear, taste, touch, and smell the world around them. They feel emotions and can be happy or sad or frightened—all depending on the information their feeling function provides, and they can even intuitively sense changes in their mother's mood. Many mothers say: "My baby knows when I'm going to go out." A child's inner experience is very real even before he or she has learned to name and describe it.

We need our functions to bring us information and to make sense of it. Our survival depends on this. For instance, without sensate awareness, we would not know if we were injured, sick, or cold. As much as we depend upon sensate awareness to maintain our health, we also depend upon our intuition to guide us safely when other information isn't available. Intuition is like the small quiet voice within that says, "don't go there."

Our feeling function helps us to determine not only the mood in a room, but also if what we are experiencing is pleasing or distasteful, sad or joyful. The emotions we experience through our feeling function help us to know who and what we are, and what is good for us and what is not. Our ability to empathize with others depends on our feeling function along with our other functions.

We weigh our feelings, attend to our intuitive sense of the situation at hand, and note the sensations our body reveals. In fact, because our feelings, intuition, and sensations give us knowledge that we actually experience, they are our primary sources of information.

Different from this direct experience is a secondary source of information: thinking. We form abstract concepts about our experience or about information presented to us. We most obviously depend upon our thinking function to reason, assimilate, and make sense of the information we get from our other three functions which, when fully working, provide us with a rich inner world that works in harmony with the outer world.

Disconnection from any of our functions can result from a number of causes: chemical imbalance, illness, and even a severe blow to the head. With certain illnesses, such as Alzheimer's disease, biological and neurological "connections" shut down and the afflicted person loses memory and eventually awareness of other mental and bodily functions. But a great many people to some degree lose the use of some of their functions because they have been trained to disconnect.

Training to Disconnect

When Jack was three years old his parents, Dick and Jane, with the best of intentions, took him into town to get him some winter clothes. After an hour of stops and starts they hurried out of a store to get some lunch. By chance, Jack, who seemed tired, fell down, injured his knee, and began to cry.

His parents said almost simultaneously as they pulled him

up, "You're not hurt. You have nothing to cry about. You're just trying to get attention, wasting time and causing a scene." Each of these statements invalidated Jack's perceptions and was the *opposite* of the truth. Jack's experience was presented to him *backwards*. An inner occurrence, his experience, was defined from outside of himself by his parents.

Jack recovered from his fall. But if this was the way Jack was often treated, how might he have experienced himself? How might he have defined himself?

If we "take in" someone else's definition of us, we believe that their definition is more *real* than our own. We substitute our self-definition with someone else's. We come to "know" ourselves in a backwards way, from the outside in, not the inside out.

If Jack, at the time of the shopping incident, took in his parents' definition of him, he would have believed that the pain in his knee was either not real or shouldn't be happening: "I'm not hurt." *He would lose some sensate awareness.* He would believe that the tears coming from his eyes were a betrayal: "I've nothing to cry about." *He would lose emotional awareness.* And he would believe he did something very bad: "I'm trying to get attention." *He would lose his intuitive awareness* that something bad was happening to him. In this way he would be trained to believe the opposite of the truth.

If he took in his parents' definitions of his experience, he would have had to discard his own. He would feel very guilty for "making" them angry, and he would also feel that he, himself, was utterly rejected. After all, to a child, he *is* his experience.

Although the following interaction took place between a parent and child, similar interactions often occur between adults.

A woman I'll call Betty walked into a café where I was having coffee with a friend. She was accompanied by her daughter, whom I'll call Suzy, about seven years old.

"What kind of ice cream do you want?" asked Betty, as they looked over the flavors laid out in tubs below the glass-topped counter.

"Mom, I want vanilla," said Suzy.

"Have chocolate chip," said her mother.

"No. I'll have vanilla."

"You'd like chocolate-walnut better."

"No. I want vanilla."

"You don't want vanilla. I know you prefer some kind of chocolate," said her mother.

"I want vanilla."

"You don't want vanilla."

"Yes I do."

"Well, aren't you a strange one," said her mother.

As the conversation progressed the mother's statements seemed more and more strange to me. They had an odd, backwards quality about them. Betty could only know her own likes and dislikes, not her daughter's. Betty was acting as if she knew what Suzy wanted.

Since Suzy's personal reality was negated, she was invited to ignore herself. She was actually told that what she knew from within—her preference—was wrong and that what she heard from without—her mother's conjecture—was right. She also heard that her authentic self (the one that wanted vanilla) was not acceptable to her mother.

While Betty appeared to have had a good intention, to buy her daughter some delicious ice cream, she was in fact assaulting her daughter's psychic boundary.

How much influence did Betty's words carry? Whose reality was whose? Whose taste was whose? Whose desire was whose? And who was acting strangely? Is there something "backwards" about Betty's behavior?

Nevertheless, Suzy did not take in her mother's definition of her; she seemed able to withstand the small assaults. She wasn't persuaded that her mother knew her inner reality better than she knew it herself. But many young girls would succumb to the authority of a parent. It is likely that if Suzy's mother believed that she could define her daughter in terms of her taste and choices, this was not her first attempt.

Given her mother's persistence, it is impressive that Suzy maintained her sense of self and her clear vision of her personal preferences. It is highly probable that someone who was a strong influence in Suzy's life validated and affirmed her inner reality.

Without consistent affirmation, it is easy for a child to take in a parent's definition of his or her inner reality. As you may recall, a child's boundaries are open to receive nurturing protection. To the child, his or her parents are godlike. But these gods, if not aware of themselves, may make up some things and leave others undone. Fabrication and neglect in certain contexts can even perplex many adults.

Nature itself doesn't work in a backwards way. Even a plant grows from the inside out, fed by the earth and sustained by the sun. Plants know exactly what they need to grow. And they go looking for it. They turn toward the sun and send searching roots into the earth. Children similarly turn to their parents to get what they need to grow. It is the earth's own gravitational pull that instructs a plant as to what is "up" and what is "down." Parents, by example, are in effect the "gravitational pull" for the child, exemplifying the boundaries, not of up and down, but of right and wrong, real and unreal.

Jack's parents confused what was real with what was not real. They completely disregarded the truth of Jack's experience. With seemingly small and common messages, such as "You're not hurt," Jack was being trained to distrust himself. He was learning to disconnect from his feelings, his sensations, even his intuitive sense of what was happening. If he lost all trust in himself, he might even disconnect from his thinking and base his choices and actions solely on someone else's thinking, or on what he was told without critical evaluation. Or he may even refuse to think about something at all and may base his actions solely on a feeling, possibly anger, regardless of what his thinking may tell him.

In the same way that Betty acted as if she knew what Suzy wanted, Jack's parents, Dick and Jane, acted as if they knew their child's experience. They acted as if they could enter his psychic boundary and know his personal reality—the unknowable. They seemed not to find it strange to do so, because they didn't even notice that what they were doing was nonsensical. Their behavior had a backwards quality to it. Did Jack's parents believe that they knew his experience? How else could they presume to define it?

Isn't it senseless to tell someone that *what* they are experiencing *isn't* what they are experiencing? What is more real than our own experience? If I feel fear, I feel fear.

Since Dick and Jane intended to be good parents, what could wrest them from their empathy for their own child? Were they under the influence of a spell? If they were, did Jack fall under the spell too? I think not yet. But, he was learning to close the gate on his inner experience and to open the gate on its opposite: a very distorted reflection of who and what he was. He was still in touch with himself, however, and if not too severely traumatized, he might remain aware of his inner experience, though be somewhat confused and unsure of himself and his choices.

As children mature they learn to sort out their experiences, to name them, to think about them, to attribute meaning to them. But, if they become "disconnected" from themselves, they lose this valuable knowledge.

Just as we can only see ourselves clearly in an undistorted mirror, so, too, we can best see our inner reality when it is reflected back to us without distortion. Children who are nurtured, supported, and clearly mirrored by their caretakers can "see" themselves clearly.

A distortion occurs whenever one person defines another person. For instance, if I said, "I'm hungry," and someone reflected that information back to me in a backwards way by saying, "You aren't hungry. It wasn't that long ago that you ate," they would be presenting a distortion to me. I would feel as if I had looked in a fun house mirror. I would see my inner reality reflected to me in a strange and backwards way. Being defined backwards often has extraordinary ramifications.

Because we have not understood psychic boundaries, indeed, have only very recently begun to understand the psyche, some people have come to normalize the very odd behavior that assumes one person has access to another person's inner reality.

Even when our parents reflect our reality accurately to us, other circumstances can influence us to disconnect from ourselves. We may find that we are beside ourselves when we would rather not be. Our family or culture may rigidly proscribe limits to our expression and action. "You're too old for that." "Don't do too much." "Toughen up."

All disconnection is a matter of degree. The following are some examples of how children may be trained to narrow their experience and limit their awareness by being defined backwards.

A girl may be defined as "delicate." A boy may be defined as a "little toughie." A girl may be defined as feminine only when she doesn't run, jump, or climb. A boy may be defined as masculine only if he runs, jumps, and climbs.

In childhood, we depend upon others to reflect our personal experience back to us. We learn to describe and accept it when it is accurately named by another. For example, "It looks like you're hurt, let's see," said with empathy, gives a name and meaning to our experience. We then can give it conscious thought. Otherwise we would not know what to think of our experience. We might even experience mistreatment as normal.

A client who wasn't disconnected from himself, but was very sad, made sense of his feelings when he understood how his parents, being both verbally and physically abusive to him, had controlled him. Although he hadn't known that he was abused, he had never been dissuaded of his feelings. Unlike Jack he stayed connected to himself, even to his sadness.

His was an extreme case. He had been so isolated in childhood that he hadn't known what, if anything, had been wrong. Not having had a place to stand apart, to gain perspective to see what was wrong, thirty years after the fact, he said, "I'm only just beginning to realize about the way I grew up."

"How was that?" I asked.

"That it wasn't right the way I was brought up. I wasn't allowed in the house. I slept in the shed—did the work and I was only a child. How could I have known anything different? I thought it was normal.

"I know I've got a lot of healing to do, but my heart's been touched. I can't describe the feeling. I know I can love and I am loved so I know I'll get to the place where I will know myself."

Besides being trained to disconnect, a person may *try* to disconnect.

Trying to Disconnect

When a child is constantly defined by a parent, he or she endures an ongoing sense of rejection. Because this abuse is so painful, and the child's need to be accepted is so great, he or she may attempt to gain the rejecting parent's love and acceptance by emulating his or her behavior. If this occurs, the child will *try* not to feel, not only to escape his painful feelings of total rejection, but also to be acceptable to the parent who doesn't show feelings or who puts down people who do show them.

A male child will also be more inclined to try to emulate those men who don't show emotions, like the ones in movies and on television who never seem to cry. Similarly, if he is told intuition is a "girl-thing," he will try to ignore his intuition. He will also look to his father for approval of his "manliness" and so try not to notice physical pain if his father doesn't seem to notice it.

In this way children try to *disconnect* themselves from the information they would receive from their feeling, intuitive, and sensate functions. Even as adults these patterns usually persist and the person so afflicted continues to lose awareness.

I once talked with a man who asked very seriously, "What is the difference between pain and anger?"

He had called for help with his temper, because he realized that he yelled at his wife, putting her down when she talked on the phone, worked at her bookkeeping, or did anything that kept her from giving him attention right when he wanted it. He was so disconnected from himself, that he was unable to feel the pain of his loss when she was unavailable to him. He was clearly a man who had never been allowed to grieve his losses in childhood. As a matter of fact, the only feeling he seemed able to identify was anger.

Trauma and Disconnection

Aside from training to disconnect, trying to disconnect, and specific biological losses of mental capability due to disease or injury, we may lose awareness through trauma.

When our feelings or sensations are very painful we may disconnect from them, that is, have no conscious experience of them. This can occur in an automatic way when we are severely emotionally traumatized by an unbearable event—one that comes out of nowhere.

In this case, the emotional impact is an assault to our psyche and is more than we can process. We may only recall bits and pieces of the traumatic event. Over time, most events can be integrated and we can cope with the reality of what has happened. But if we suffer frequent traumas, we may feel disorganized, stirred up inside, or dismantled whenever we are reminded of the incident.

Girls are not often *trained* to lose awareness of their feeling, sensate, intuitive, and thinking functions, because our culture allows girls and women to use all of their functions. They are allowed to have feelings. Being able to cry and to experience and express feelings is even thought of by many as not just a human attribute, but as a feminine one. Likewise, females are usually allowed a wide range of sensate experiences. They are aware of delicate and complex sensations and attend to the pain of bruises and blows. They are allowed to be intuitive. Additionally, they are encouraged to use their intellect (thinking function). In fact, more women than men are entering college in the United States these days.[1] Consequently, girls are not as likely as boys to *try* to lose awareness.

When women are disconnected, the knife that severs them from themselves is usually one of trauma, sharp and yet so lasting that it can hardly have cut quickly or cleanly. Of course, men, too, often suffer this depth of trauma. After serving in wars, for instance, they often experience periodic trauma throughout their lives.

Cultural Mandates to Disconnect

Our sense of self develops naturally throughout our lives. But this natural process may be restricted by our cultural beliefs.

The people with whom you come in contact and the culture in which you live, its stories, myths, institutions, dogmas, and traditions, may subtly define you, just as if someone, anyone but you, knew who you were and how you should be.

Disconnection gets the upper hand in many people's lives. Some people not only have lost their connections to their feelings, sensations, and intuitions through training, trying, and trauma, but also have fallen under the influence of collective values, traditions, and expectations that foster disconnection. This mandate to disconnect has developed in two primary ways.

First, to bring about civilization in the world, people have had to focus outside of themselves to attend to the community needs in the world around them. Consequently they've paid little or no attention to their inner experience, have even lost touch with it.

Second, some people, under the influence of cultural expectations, have learned to tune out their inner experience. From the beginnings of human history, despite fear, despite their intuitive sense that death was probable, despite physical pain, people have heroically protected their homes and lands from foreign invaders. But after thousands of years some learned not to feel or attend to their inner experience at all. What was temporarily necessary became for some the norm, even outside of the battlefield.

Not attending to one's inner experience was at first a necessary discipline, but it eventually became a deeply ingrained pattern of self-negation closely tied to identity and thought to be a strength. People were trained in *not-knowing* by people in authority. Assuming authority over another person's inner experience has a long history. It is as old as hierarchy itself.

Inner awareness was purged from those who stood as surrogates for an earlier generation who could no longer take up arms nor trek to a distant land. Generation after generation fostered disconnection and then forgot why.

Carrying the goal of disconnection to the extreme, some members of the United States military made headlines when they tested their skill at disowning their sensate function by sticking pins into themselves and each other. Some non-military people have done similar exercises. Some groups have not only made disconnection valorous, but also have attempted to normalize this aberration.

If disconnection and mutual abuse has taken hold in military training, in gangs, in initiations and hazings, could it also be that some people have unconsciously wanted to share the horror of their own training to disconnect? Additionally, if you can abuse your own side with impunity, how much more readily will you abuse the enemy of the day?

"We are tough." (Our sensate experience is blocked.) "We can take it." (Our emotional experience is blocked.) "We only look at the cold hard facts." (Our intuition is blocked)

Some Outcomes

If we are taught to doubt ourselves, or to distrust inner knowledge in general, we may pay no attention to this knowledge. We may hardly notice sensate experience: "How did I get that bruise?" Or block our feelings: "I've never liked this kind of work, so why did I take this job?" Or disregard an intuitive warning: "I knew I shouldn't have gone in there." Tragically, this was the training that Jack, who angrily demanded his coat from his wife, received.

Just one generation ago, when Jack's parents were children, they were also, on many occasions, defined by others. In her childhood, Jack's mother, Jane, felt just as Jack had felt when he'd hurt himself—betrayed by herself, that somehow something was wrong with her experience. She was unheard and unseen except when she performed perfectly. As an adult she was unsure of herself. There was a possibility, however, that she would eventually develop a deeper and clearer awareness of herself. She had a particular advantage, because she lived in a culture that supported the development of not only her intellectual gifts, but also her ability to know and express her feelings. And she wasn't expected to ignore her sensate experience and her intuitive knowledge. Culturally, she was allowed to know herself. However, a severe trauma could lessen even that advantage.

Jack's father, Dick, had also learned to distrust himself and his own experience. His culture, while supporting him in developing his intellect, trained him to be "tough," to ignore many signals from himself. He learned to close the gate on many experiences that gave him information about himself. He learned to disconnect.

How could he feel sad about his neighbor's distress? Wasn't competition a man's game? How could he sense what Jack needed from him? Wasn't intuition a woman's game? How could he let a little chest pain stop him? Wasn't backing off a shameful act?

The Self-Defining Child

When the truth of our being is clearly reflected to us, we know ourselves and trust ourselves. Our self-knowledge is enhanced and we remain connected to ourselves. We then have the ability, like Suzy and like the woman who glued the book back together, to recognize and resist controlling behavior.

In contrast to Jack's training to disconnect, imagine a child who had not been defined backwards, i.e., from the outside in. He would define himself in accordance with his experience. His experience would be acknowledged and its clear reflection would validate him. He would know himself. He would know his own feelings, motives, intuitions, and sensations. He would be able to describe them, and he would know that they were real.

At different times he might feel, for example, respectful, strong, courageous, undaunted, creative, expressive, intelligent, curious, sad, angry, excited, competent, trusting, or uncertain. Nothing would hold him back from knowing himself. Nothing would restrain him from sharing his warmth and himself with others.

He wouldn't have to hold back his tears, or hold back his enthusiasm, in order to be the way his parents imagined him to be. He wouldn't have to meet their needs in a backwards way. They would meet his. In this way he would know himself, what he felt, what he could endure, and the meaning of his experience.

People who have been treated in backwards ways, who have been told what they want, what they feel, and so forth, who haven't had their experience clearly reflected back to them, are usually unsure of their experience, or what it means. They are, to some degree, disconnected from themselves. How then do they develop their identity? If they are beside themselves most of the time, how do they know their own nature? How do they define themselves? Which "self" would one bring to a relationship or to the world if he or she was in fact disconnected from his or her true self?

Chapter VII

Built Backwards

*In childhood they were our gods,
but even gods do not define us.*

T here is only one way to build an identity if one is discon- nected from one's inner reality, and that is to create one from the outside in, backwards.

Sadly, but understandably, when people have undergone a long training in disconnection and have successfully learned to close the gate on most of their feelings, sensations, and intu- itions, they will make themselves up according to what they *think* they are, what they would like to be, and, most especially, what they've been told they are or are not.

Having learned to deny their own wisdom and having taken in other people's definitions of them, without even realizing it, those who are disconnected from themselves construct an iden- tity not grounded in experience but constructed out of, or in reaction to, other people's ideas, expectations, and values.

Their opinions, fears, beliefs, likes, and dislikes, rather than being experientially based—the result of a slow maturation process that develops through life experience—are acquired from others, often according to, or in opposition to, parental and cultural dictates. The outcome is an identity built backwards.

When people unwittingly form their identity out of one imposed on them by others, *how they appear to others* becomes an all-important barometer by which to validate their existence. In a backwards construction of self, there is no three-dimensionality, no depth, no space for future evolution and integration with the world. Human empathy, warmth, allowance for error—all that is considered to be humanity itself—may find no niche, no accommodation.

People are most likely to accept others' definitions of them when they are young, even if there is a great discrep- ancy between their own experience and what they are told they are experiencing.

A person can be influenced to build his or her identity back- wards in many ways. For instance, if the budding philosopher is convinced he is, and must be, a farmer like his father, he will suppress his intellect and curiosity about life. His identity will become a fragile construction of mind disconnected from his nature, his talents, and his inclinations.

Alternatively, some people suffer being defined by someone else while remaining aware of their own feelings, sensations, and intuitions. In this way they retain self-knowledge but bear the pain of nonacceptance.

A woman described to me how difficult her childhood had been. Unlike the man who as a child was forced to live in a shed, she knew, even when she was very young, that the way she was treated was wrong. She was not isolated as he had been, so she was able to understand that her life was different from her classmates.

In childhood her father told her she was worthless and frequently punished her for her independent views. Her mother, who years later was diagnosed as mentally ill, constantly accused her of trying to make her look bad and ruining her life.

Even as a child, this woman was gifted with an inner strength. She listened to her intuition when it told her she had reason to fear her parents. She noticed how her body clenched when she was around them, even when she tried to tell herself they really loved her. Ultimately, by trusting herself, she rejected her parents' definitions of her. They were unable to keep their control over her. And, most extraordinarily, she managed to leave home at age thirteen. She found a place to stay and an after-school job. She not only built her identity from the inside out, but also, because of the challenges she had met, she knew herself very well.

People who have managed to retain their individuality despite the fact that someone tried to control them by defining them, knew that the other was pretending, they knew that the other was falsely defining them.

As we have seen, people have the ability to build their identity backwards, from an outside source, by accepting definitions of themselves that have not come from within, and by believing the pretender knew them better than they knew themselves. It is often very difficult to believe in oneself, especially when one is constantly told not to. But it is the ability and freedom to define oneself, and to see the other as pretending that protects one from negating his or her true self.

Chapter VIII

Pretending
and Its Impact

---

*Only in the theater can anyone
else define you. In real life if
someone casts you in a role of
their own making, they are
playing "let's pretend."*

I f someone defines you, even in subtle ways, they are *pretending* to know the unknowable. There is a quality of fantasy to their words and sometimes to their actions. Even so, they are usually unaware of the fact that they are playing "let's pretend." They fool themselves and sometimes others into thinking that what they are saying is true or that what they are doing is right.

When people "make up" your reality—*as if they were you*—they are trying to control you, even when they don't realize it.

When people attempt to control you they begin by pretending. When they define you they are acting in a senseless way. They are pretending. When people act as if you do not exist or are not a real person with a reality of your own—as did the miller—they are pretending. In this subtle and often *unconscious* way, they are attempting to exert control over you—your space, time, resources, or even your life.

We know that they are pretending because in actual fact, no one can tell you what you want, believe, should do, or why you have done what you have done. No one can know your inner reality, your intentions, your motives, what you think, believe, feel, like, dislike, what you know, how you do what you do, or who you are. If someone does pretend to know your inner reality: "You're trying to start a fight," they have it *backwards*. People can only know themselves. It doesn't work the other way around.

Since only you can define yourself, your self-definition is yours. It isn't necessary that you prove it or explain it. It is, after all, your own. Self-definition is inherent in being a person.

Despite the evidence, it is difficult for many people to realize that the person who defines them is not being rational. They feel inclined to defend themselves as if the person defining them were rational. But by trying to defend themselves against someone's definitions, they are acknowledging those definitions as valid, that they make sense, when they are, in fact, complete nonsense. In Chapter 28 I will discuss ways to respond to outside definitions and attacks.

Recall how May tried to defend herself when Dee told her that she really *did* remember her birthday: "No, honestly," said May. But if she had said something else like "Cut it out," she would have given no credence to Dee's fantasy.

We know that Dee was *pretending* to know May's inner reality—her thinking, her memory, her mind. But what is really interesting is that Dee said, "You're just pretending. . . ." to May. Again, Dee had it backwards!

Millions of people try to defend themselves from abuse and describe the altercations as arguments. Are they? I think not. I see them more as a struggle to retain one's own reality when someone else has stepped into it.

Understanding this is important because it is often very confusing for everyone involved: "We get into arguments and I never know why," people often say. And when I ask, "What were you arguing about?" the answer is usually, "I don't know."

It is not always easy to spot controlling behaviors because we may believe the person who pretends to know our reality really has some right to define us. For example, myths, perpetuated through generations, can be taken for truth and cloud our thinking. Some myths that may prevent clear perception of controlling behaviors are: Men are most logical. Women are most wise. Church leaders are most holy. Of course, some men, women, and church leaders do fill this criteria.

If you believe that people who define you are logical or wise, you may have become blinded to their nonsense. Without realizing it, you may be under the influence of a belief that screens the truth from you. For instance, a woman may believe there is some way to *explain* to her mate that she's not "too sensitive" like he says, because she believes he is logical.

When authority figures such as experts or leaders assault us with *their* definitions of our inner reality, especially if they have good intentions, it may seem easier to believe that they are right than to realize that they not only have it backwards but also are pretending

Even long-held beliefs that seem like truths can cloud our perception of controlling behaviors. For instance, a man may believe that an older brother's criticism, "You'll never amount to anything," is somehow justified, because in childhood his older brother knew so much more than he did. Consequently, he may try to prove himself by defending himself against the criticism and changing his brother's mind—never realizing that his brother is playing "let's pretend" and has no right to define him.

What blinds people the most to controlling behavior is the belief that the person who consistently defines them truly loves them.

One of the saddest cases I've encountered was that of a woman who believed her mate loved her so much that only he could tell her the *real* truth about herself. Although she was highly intelligent (as later tests proved) and an extraordinarily gifted singer (as early evaluations noted), she thought that she was "not smart" and had an "unremarkable" voice. Married at twenty and widowed at sixty, she spent her later years grieving not the loss of her controlling husband, but the loss of that "other life" she might have lived had she not believed he loved her.

Inner certainty is hard to come by if one's own truth, one's very being, is constantly denied. As adults we are usually most affected and influenced by assaults to our psychic boundary when they are couched in an attitude of righteousness, blame, or caring by our mate or a family member.

Unless we know that people are pretending to know our inner reality when they define us, other people's definitions of us can shroud the truth, cloud perception, dim the light of awareness. If we accept them, we may come to believe that what is so is *not* so, and that what is not so *is* so. Most significant, we may then base our choices upon false beliefs about ourselves and find ourselves under someone else's control.

Under the best circumstances it is difficult to know ourselves, because we are all under the influence of prevailing beliefs and other people's expectations of us. These influences are even greater if we have learned to discount or ignore our own personal experience.

As we lose self-awareness, we lose our ability to respond to our inner needs. We may not even know what they are: "I guess I do like chocolate-walnut best."

Every time we accept someone else's definition of our own inner reality, we set aside our own experience and so lose awareness. Eventually we lose access to the information we would normally receive through our functions—information we need to make choices, to understand ourselves, and to act in the world. Our ancestors needed these functions to remain alert to the dangers of the wilds, and in today's world of increasing choices, we, too, need all of our functions.

Even with a strong sense of self, if our psychic boundary is frequently assaulted over a period of time, we may begin to feel uncertain. And, in an ever-increasing downward spiral, the more we are uncertain on the inside, the more we are inclined to accept statements from the outside.

Sometimes it is a long series of assaults that finally unravels one's trust in his or her self—the source of certainty, vitality, and creativity. Although we may be very uncertain, we are not likely to be defining others if we are engaged in the struggle to know ourselves and we remain aware of our feelings and the pain other peoples' definitions of us cause.

An all too common outcome of lost self-trust is that of having extreme difficulty in making choices: "I don't know what I *should* do."

But if people lose touch with themselves altogether, feel no pain—disconnect from themselves—they may attempt to control others. This disconnection usually occurs in childhood if the child is constantly defined. It rarely comes about in adulthood because once we reach adulthood truly connected to ourselves, only extreme trauma, for instance war, drugs, or torture, can break that connection.

The consequence of one person's disconnection, if extreme and long-term, can affect a great many people. Indeed, oppression, prejudice, and violence all have something to do with disconnection. Of course, not all people who feel beside themselves are oppressive, and not all people are beside themselves all the time. However, *when people are oppressive, they are usually attempting to control only one particular person or group*. To the "oppressed," coping with this behavior is extremely difficult. No one else seems to notice what is going on.

We have seen how some people pretend to know our inner reality, and how their declarations about our inner reality are really assaults. We have explored how these assaults can, if taken in, momentarily dislodge or disconnect us from ourselves, leaving us vulnerable to another's attempts to control us. What happens when people are assaulted over years and end up with little or no awareness of their inner worlds—when they are, in effect, disconnected? And how pervasive is the problem of disconnection? Let's find out in the next chapter.

Chapter IX

Pervasive Disconnection

*As long as there have
been wars, some men have
learned to disconnect.*

For thousands of years, millions of people have been put through training to close the gates to their inner awareness. The best-trained ended up with only one function fully working: their thinking function.

One reason for this is that the age of reason placed thinking at the top of the pedestal, though all of our functions are equally important. Each one provides us with a different kind of information. Although thinking was even used to prove a famous philosophical premise, "I think, therefore I am" (René Descartes), one might just as easily say, "I touch, therefore I am" or "I intuit, therefore I am" or "I feel, therefore I am."

We might imagine our functions to be like cylinders where a process takes place. Many people have been trained to disconnect so completely from their inner experience that they operate with only one cylinder fully working—their thinking function—instead of four cylinders: their thinking, intuitive, feeling, and sensate functions.

If these people are told, "Don't think, just take orders" and have already blocked their feelings, ignored their sensations, and denied their intuition, they make perfect robots— albeit, angry and/or depressed ones. Alternatively, if they rise to positions of power over others and *give* orders instead of taking them, they are usually not able to act in anyone's best interests.

We need all of our functions. If, for instance, we've lost the ability to access information from our feeling function, we will have a lot of trouble determining what we really like and dislike.

In weighing the pros and cons of moving to a new residence, a client said that he had only recently realized that he needed to take into account not just the safety of the streets, the quality of the transportation, and the climate in a certain area, but also how he *felt* when he actually was in that area. This was a revelation to him. This, he said, made choosing much easier.

Similarly, if we don't attend to our intuition we may find it hard to trust ourselves, and the less we trust ourselves, the more we may ignore our intuition.

People who, through training, trying, and trauma, have lost inner awareness and are, in a sense, disconnected from themselves, seem to be under a spell. Having virtually no inner world, they may easily "make up" an outer one. This world seems so real and they feel so certain as to how it all should be they may seek positions of leadership.

However, "one-cylinder" people who believe they should lead "four-cylinder" people have not yet learned the kindergarten lesson of full partnership. Even on a teeter-totter both riders must participate. People operating on one cylinder and wielding power over people operating on four cylinders always face the possibility of losing their power over others. For instance, the person they are trying to control may escape or defy them. When a one-cylinder person believes a possibility of escape is imminent, he or she will usually implement oppressive tactics.

In domestic situations these tactics might include verbal abuse, battering, or even disconnecting the phone to maintain control. A household example is that of a person who rages and demands the service of another and so defines the other as a servant. In nondomestic situations, an everyday example is an elected official or a person hired by an elected official who forgets that he or she is an employee of the people, and who acts independently of the wishes of the majority, or acts without informing the people in order to maintain control. An extreme example of a nondomestic situation is a dictator who imprisons people whose views differ from his or her own.

The concept of people operating on one to four cylinders is, of course, only a concept. People are complex beings, not machines, and it is not possible for someone to completely close down a function.

However, when people operate on one function primarily they are unaware of themselves in ordinary circumstances, and they *are,* in an important sense, beside themselves. Consequently, they do try to get a grip ion someone else just as they would do in a crisis. This is a way of being grounded when they aren't grounded in themselves.

I've asked hundreds of pretenders if they recall what they said when they defined someone. Most could not clearly remember. They seemed to be unaware of their own reality while they simultaneously acted as if they knew the reality of another person.

If Betty, in the ice cream story, were asked if she knew her daughter's inner reality better than her daughter knew it, it is most likely that Betty would say, "No." And if she were asked if she thought her daughter was strange, it's also likely she'd say, "No, of course not!"

Betty, like most people who consistently define another person, is not likely to recall her words, because Betty is beside herself when she "makes up" her daughter. How can she reflect upon her words if she is "not quite there" when she speaks? If she continued to try make choices for her daughter, but met resistance, would she become angrier and define her daughter in more harmful ways? Would she say she treated her daughter this way because she disliked her? Or would she claim that she loved her too much?

We are inclined to tolerate certain assaults because they arise out of crisis, with the perpetrators naturally being beside themselves. We recognize the circumstances around their behavior. On the other hand, we find that some people appear to be beside themselves most of the time. Often operating primarily on one cylinder, with a built-backwards identity, there is a backwards quality to their behavior. Might they approach others in a backwards way?

Chapter X

Backwards Approaches

Defining a stranger is a very bizarre thing to attempt.

P erson-to-person relationships are the foundation of the world. When these relationships are good ones, there is harmony. When these relationships are bad, there is turmoil. So, how does a person who is disconnected from him- or herself relate to people? What happens to his or her relationships? Let's take a look at how people attempt to relate to others when they have become, for the most part, disconnected from themselves.

People who operate on one cylinder, so to speak, with a built-backwards identity, are inclined to approach others in a backwards way. They may actually define a stranger as a way of introducing themselves, possibly intending to establish an instant connection. Their approach is often to tell the other what he or she should do, has done, will do, and so forth.

This is a very important discovery on our journey of exploration through the maze of senseless behavior woven into our world. In fact, I believe it to be one of the more senseless behaviors, well woven into the fabric of everyday communications. We'll spend a little time exploring this territory so that we can find everything we need to carry us through the rest of our journey.

If we see someone on a daily basis, we may assume that we know them so well that we know what they're thinking or what they should do. If we voice such an assumption, defining them in one way or another, we are likely to find out we're wrong and that our assumption calls for an apology. But, if we define a stranger, we are indulging in even more bizarre behavior without even thinking about it. Very often people do just that, approach others backwards, defining them from the outside in. We'll look at some specific backwards approaches in a moment so we can see just how strange they are.

Assuming that some people are exposed to a backwards way of relating in childhood and emulate it until it becomes a habit, it is then reasonable to assume that, if it were only a learned behavior, as hard as it is to unlearn something, these people could. Certainly a person would apologize if what they were doing were pointed out to them, if they could understand or see what they'd done, if they didn't want to look silly, act delusional, or inadvertently cause harm.

But many people find it extremely difficult to break the "habit" of defining people, whether they are strangers or not. Recall the man who asked, "Why can't I take it [his good behavior] ten minutes down the road [to his wife and family]?" He seemed to feel unable to do this. Possibly his oppressive behavior was actually more than just a habit. It seems that it had something to do with his *way of being* with his wife and family—his sense of closeness to them. Just the opposite of what one might imagine.

Let's look at some backwards approaches and see if we can see how making up another person relates to closeness, bonding, and connection. We begin our exploration by taking a close look at how someone can approach another person backwards long before a bond or connection is established.

The Smile Story

Not long ago, I was concentrating on my plans for a trip into Manhattan while I poured my morning coffee from a golden urn in the lobby of a lovely hotel near New York City. Suddenly, I heard someone who seemed to be talking to me, standing just behind me and to the right. I turned and saw a stranger. No one else was there. It must have been me to whom he was speaking.

"What?" I asked.

"Smile!"

"What?"

"SMILE, it's a NICE DAY!" he said, very emphatically.

"What?" I asked again, incredulous and taken aback.

"SMILE, it's a NICE DAY!" he said, even more emphatically.

Nearly speechless, I said, "Whaaat?" again. I couldn't take it in. It somehow didn't make sense. What he was saying had nothing to do with me. My mind was filled with thoughts of the public transportation schedule and directions to the bus and how close the drop-off point was to my desired destination.

As I stood there, another, "Whaaaat?" still lingering on my lips, he stopped his loud demands and walked away. I had noticed that his name tag showed that he was a member of the convention I'd spoken to the day before.

I thought, possibly he thought he knew me. Possibly he was trying to connect with me by telling me to smile, as if the expression on my face should be different; as if he were privy to my thoughts and feelings and knew what it should be, as if he could define me, as if this made him closer to me, as if defining me were a way of connecting.

Did the stranger who had demanded my smile believe that he was or could be so close to me he could tell me how to be? So close that, in a harmless but *backwards* way, he was privy to my inner reality?

As innocuous as his approach was, it was one I could not emulate. I had never approached a stranger, or even someone I knew well, and demanded a smile.

The very next morning, in the same hotel, another interesting event unfolded.

The "You Read Too Much" Story

In a restaurant, several people left a table not far from the table where I was sitting reading a newspaper while eating breakfast. Very strangely, like the morning before, I suddenly heard someone talking to me, just behind me, but this time to the left. "What?" I asked, looking up to meet the gaze of another stranger.

"YOU READ TOO MUCH," he said brusquely.

"Whaaaaat?!?" I asked, more incredulously than the morning before.

"YOU READ TOO MUCH," he repeated awkwardly.

"Whaaat?" I asked again, while I struggled to grasp the meaning of this man's strange declaration.

Seeming to have embarrassed himself, he mumbled something like "they're up ahead" and headed off after "them." I saw his name tag, though, and realized that he also was a member of the convention where I'd spoken.

Possibly he, too, was trying to connect with me by telling me that I read too much—as if what I was doing (compared to what?) was excessive, as if we were "so close" he were privy to my thoughts, feelings, even to my reading habits, and knew what I *should* be doing, as if he could define me. *As if defining me were a way of connecting.*

What would explain these strange approaches?

In both instances I was told something about my inner reality before I was asked about it.

It seems that some unaware, well-meaning, hard-working people, while intending to connect with us, may instead do the opposite. When trying to make a connection, or strike up a conversation, or get to know us, they approach us backwards.

People disconnect from us the moment they begin to define us. They begin to connect with us when they define themselves to us or ask us about ourselves. That's how we get to know them and how they get to know us. It doesn't work the other way around.

For instance, I might have had a conversation with the man who said, "You read too much," if he'd, instead, said something like, "Excuse me if I'm interrupting. I'm _____. I heard your talk and was wondering about ____. Do you have a minute?"

I don't think these two strangers meant to startle me or throw me off balance. They simply acted as if they could define me.

In the first case, I didn't explain why I wasn't smiling, and in the second I didn't defend the fact that I was reading. But if I had, wouldn't I have given the impression that someone could connect with me, but in a backwards way? Wouldn't I have given tacit approval of another person's taking one tiny step across my psychic boundary?

Wouldn't my explanation or defense suggest to the intruder that he was right in thinking, "We're so close. I know how she should be because she is, in fact, explaining why in *this* case she doesn't agree. Her explanation suggests that in *some* cases I *do* know how she should be."

Could a subtle step across a boundary be a way to check out the possibility of a bigger step? Many times I have heard people reflect upon a poor relationship, saying, "If only I'd seen those little signals and recognized them for what they were—a glimpse of the controlling personality."

I told the "You Read Too Much" story to a woman who had once been in a battering relationship. She had been in training for many years to question herself. Even now, after several years of freedom, when she heard my story she said, "If right now I heard, 'You read too much!' I would either have wondered if I did or wondered why I gave the impression that I did."

Even when a person isn't told what is "wrong with" them or how they "should be," they may be defined in an even more subtle manner. A client told me that he found that he was constantly explaining himself to a seemingly loving mate who, though adamant about her affections, paradoxically claimed to know his every motive. Furthermore, she objected to all his attempts to define himself.

Speaking of his wife, he gave the following account.

> *Yesterday she said, "You bought that print because of the colors."*
>
> *I said, "No, I saw it as a study in contrasts."*
>
> *Then she said, "I know the colors are your favorites. You just like to argue."*
>
> *Of course, I objected. I told her I hate arguing. The whole thing turns my stomach. I feel like I am under constant attack, and that I have to explain my position on everything.*
>
> *When I was reading last night, she said, "You sure go for female sleuths."*
>
> *I said, "That's not it," and explained that I'd just finished a mystery last week that had a male detective and that I just enjoy mysteries.*
>
> *Why can't she show some interest in me? Why can't she ask me what I like best about a painting, for example. Or a book for that matter. I feel like I'm drowning in her definitions of me. Almost like I have to explain my very existence.*

In relationships people usually try to explain themselves so that their "significant other" will know them. But this particular significant other approached her partner backwards.

People who find themselves in similar circumstances often believe that people who define them are rational and simply have made an assumption and will stop making assumptions as soon as they're told that their assumptions are false. This works with some people, but to a person whose identity is built backwards, explanations carry only the message, "In this case you are wrong. It *is* okay to define me but not in this particular way." They act as if defining others is justified, rational, and not part of a "let's pretend" world.

When I was told on one occasion to "smile" and on another that I "read too much," I wasn't influenced to wonder if I should be different—smile more or read less—nor did I suffer harm, nor did I explain myself. I was too surprised to do so. On the other hand, as bizarre as the comments were, if they had been made by a family member, I might have thought I could explain how inappropriate they were so that he or she would better understand me.

Although backwards approaches may seem a small thing, easy to deal with, nothing compared to violence, gangs, and other pressing relationship issues, a backwards approach is like a whiff of smoke from a distant fire, something we may ignore until it is so close that it threatens to consume us.

Backwards approaches at best reveal fuzzy thinking and at worst create devastating problems. I have found that people who cannot accept, feel, or even conceptualize their inner experience not only make themselves up from the outside in but also approach others in the same way, making *them* up from the outside in, *not even noticing that they are doing so.*

While anyone may, in moments of forgetfulness, tell another person who, what, or how they are or *should* be or what they *should* do, I have met people in every walk of life who do this as a matter of course. People who say such things as, "Men are all . . ." or "Women should . . ." These statements define nearly half the world's population all at once.

I remember, in my own childhood, a neighbor who defined people. When she would see what appeared to be a student on her way to the local college, she would say, "Humph. Well doesn't she think she's smart, going to college!"

It seems a silly thing to do. Why is this kind of behavior so common that people who indulge in it don't seem embarrassed?

Is it "just the way it is," that people defining people is to be expected—not worth further thought? I think not. I believe that it is worth our consideration because it is of consequence to every one of us. Other people's definitions of us are not just absurd—if unchallenged, they erect prison walls around us. As they rise higher, the light of awareness fades. The world darkens. We lose freedom, safety, confidence, conviction, and sometimes ourselves.

In the very act of defining another person, one unconsciously plays God. At the extreme, don't people who play tyrant, despot, dictator, or oppressor play God? Playing God is not uncommon and it is not always noticed. We have yet to see a world in which people do not make up people. We have not even come close.

The consequences of disconnection are many and profound. They are pertinent to our problems—our daily struggles to live in a world of justice and freedom. *They are problematic for a person who, after being disconnected from his or her self, wants to connect with another person.*

Chapter XI

Backwards Connections

The unknowable about another is everything that exists behind their psychic boundary.

W hen people approach others backwards, they are, most likely, attempting to connect backwards. A backwards connection is just the opposite of a real connection, which is based upon two people relating to each other. A backwards connection is just a small step away from where control of the other is the (often unconscious) objective.

A backwards connection begins with an assumption or definition of the other that ends all possibility of a relationship, at least in that interaction. It may be initiated with the intention of getting "closer" to another person, or with the intention of attacking the other. For example, once Sydney defines Lee— "You've always got to be right"—Sydney cannot relate to Lee because the real Lee no longer exists in Sydney's mind.

Recall Jack's parents. When they denied Jack's reality and defined him by telling him what he experienced, they could neither hear nor see the real Jack. They seemed to want him to be a different child, one that was not hurt and did not express pain. It was as if the only child they would accept was a pretend child. They were rejecting their real child and relating to their pretend child. Consequently they could not relate to Jack.

Connecting backwards is a kind of sick self-help program—an automatic and false way of connecting that keeps one from having to accept the reality of another person. In contrast, a real connection is an empathetic one that allows one person to see and to hear the other.

The first sign of a backwards connection is a backwards approach. If the approach is accepted, or cannot be avoided, as in a parent-to-child or dictator-to-citizen relationship, the connection is made.

If, for instance, I had defended my reading schedule when I was defined as "reading too much," I would have been addressing the defining statement rather than the stranger's behavior. Inadvertently I would have accepted a backwards approach and, therefore, allowed his backwards connection to me. I would have been putting across the idea that the process of defining me was *okay*, but the content, the definition, was *wrong*. Even when one does not accept a backwards approach or connection, some perpetrators persist in attempting to establish one.

Since "making people up" involves an assumption about another person, we can think of this assumption as a preconceived idea, a vision of the other. For instance, some people have an idea-picture of "grandmother." When they think "grandmother," they imagine an older woman with curly white hair piled on top of her head, wearing glasses and an apron. They don't, for instance, imagine a tall, glamorous woman with long dark hair who happens to be a grandmother.

Another example is when in love, some people envision a traditional picture of a prince or princess. It seems to hover over their chosen one, and they see this person through the lens of this vision, just as if they were looking through special colored glasses that filter out all but his or her finest qualities and even potentials. Part of "being in love" is seeing the best about the other as well as one's own best self reflected in their eyes.

It is well known that a girl may think of her boyfriend as heroic and valiant, or a that a boy may think of his girlfriend as a special being filled with mystery and allure.

Generally, as relationships develop, these "pictures" are tempered with reality. Mature people recall these youthful visions. In a mature relationship, each person sees the other's desirable and less desirable qualities, as well as their limitations. They are able to see their partner as a whole person. The glamorous vision is modified through time and maturation. The real person emerges, and the relationship grows ever more interesting.

Real problems arise if an illusion remains—a collection of thoughts that displace one's mate in such a way that he or she cannot be seen at all. In relationships, our openness to others' individuality allows us get to know them and become closer to them.

The following poem reveals the reality of an illusory picture of the "other." It was sent by a man to his former fiancée.

Your beauty fills my waking dreams
I love it all and all it means.
I always have and always will,
Even now I love it still.
It made me glad to hold you near
How could you just disappear?
I am certain that my claim
Requires you to remain.
All my future, oh, so bright
Turned into a lonely night.
What should be with me for life
Is lost without my promised wife.
Now my meaning, purpose, feeling
Have been taken. Fate is stealing.
But I can never let it be.
This I know. This I see.
I love your beauty, always had.
It's just senseless. It's so sad
You're the best I could find.
Why couldn't we be just one mind?

I have spoken to many people who thought their mate was of one mind with them. I've found that of all the illusions people have about others, the most common and the most devastating to any kind of relationship is the idea of being of one mind with one's mate. This illusion opens the door for a Pretend Person to be mistaken for a real person.

The Pretend Person

I invite you to imagine what it would be like to be in the company of someone whose vision of you was so overwhelming that from their perspective *you* do not exist, you can't be heard or seen.

Figuratively speaking, their image of you is that of a Pretend Person who doesn't just float over you like a vision, shaping their perception of you, but instead drifts into you. It would be as if they had extended a tentacle from their mind into yours—trespassing your psychic boundary, anchoring in you. If this occurred, a backwards connection would have been established. Not surprisingly, they may claim to know you better than you know yourself.

This anchoring in the other occurs quite frequently in couple relationships. It is a way of connecting backwards to another person. I have heard from thousands of people who describe this very experience. Generally, they say that in the beginning of their relationship they got along very well. They talked over problems, shared their thoughts and concerns, and, just as one would expect in a good relationship, they came to easy and happy agreements, and were able to resolve misunderstandings and make joint decisions. Then quite suddenly everything changed. Their mate seemed to change almost overnight, switching from being able to hear and respond to them, to not seeming to be able to see or hear them at all.

When this switch occurs in couple relationships, if it doesn't occur in the first weeks of the relationship, it takes place when there is a significant change in the circumstances surrounding the relationship. For instance, it may occur when the couple becomes engaged to marry, or when they begin living together, or on the day of marriage, or on their honeymoon, or when one person leaves a job to stay home with a child.

We might ask: Why does a change in circumstance surrounding the relationship trigger a switch in one of the partners from healthy behavior to controlling behavior? The one common factor to any change that triggers the switch is that the perpetrator feels *more secure*. His or her mate is not likely to leave, not now that they're engaged, living together, married, or having a child. All along the Pretender was unconsciously looking for a safe harbor for his or her dream person.

Pretenders don't anchor their Pretend Persons in their mates unless they believe that the body they are anchoring in is not likely to leave them. This is the security they are looking for and, although anchoring a Pretend Person in a real person is an unconscious process on the part of the Pretender, it is often easy to pinpoint the event that triggers it. The following example illustrates this phenomenon.

> *A woman called me in deep distress. She'd been married for sixteen years, and she was coping with a husband who either ignored her or was angry and overtly abusive. But the first half of the marriage, she told me, wasn't like that at all.*
>
> *"Do you have a child about eight years old?" I asked.*
>
> *"How did you know?" she said.*
>
> *"If you had a job and quit it to stay home, that action would have triggered the switch," I said.*
>
> *She said that she had quit her job to raise her child.*

Looking through the lens presented in this book, I could see that when she became more dependent on her husband, he felt secure, because she wasn't likely to get away. He then let his Pretend Person, dream woman, drift into her, so to speak.

I don't think that this woman's husband could have consciously realized that he had anchored his dream woman in her. Instead, as often happens, I believe he felt comfortable enough to stop seeing his wife as a person who was "out there," who required his attention. As one man put it, he simply relaxed and the dream woman must have just slipped in.

To avoid this backwards connection and others, it is very important to notice backwards approaches. Backwards connections may not seem particularly disastrous at first glance, "He thinks I'm a princess" or "She thinks I'm a prince." However, once they take place, if not reversed quickly (and that's not always possible), the person who connects to you this way is only one tiny step away from establishing a Control Connection to you. We'll explore Control Connections a little later.

A middle-aged man, successful in the worldly sense, described his growing up. As he learned about the concept of the pretend person, he said that he did have a dream person when he was very little. She was like an inner voice that said, "You're great, you're fine."

And, yes, she was always there. She was like his inner "need-meeter." As he got older, this dream person became his dream girl. I could see that he had come to believe that he'd get a real walking and talking girl someday just like his dream girl.

One day he knew he really wanted this dream girl. As he got a little older, he said he learned from songs and movies and other guys what he would have to do to get one.

"I'd have to go on dates, pay for things, or bring presents or flowers and say nice things," he said.

He set out in earnest to find the right body for his dream girl. "I even tried to find out the measurements of different girls," he said.

He was on the lookout for a "good body." He did all the things he thought he was supposed to do, and sure enough he got his dream girl. By then, she was his dream *woman*.

The dream girl that becomes the dream woman is like the personification of a man's feminine side—the unconscious part, the part that contains his "unacceptable" feelings, intuitions, and sensations. He connects to this hidden part of himself in earliest childhood instead of connecting to his real self because it "holds" so much of his experience.

Conversely, for a woman, a dream man may be thought of as the personification of a woman's undeveloped or masculine side—assertive and active. This kind of dream person occurs less frequently than it did in the past, because women (in our culture) have been able to be more assertive and active than they were even fifty years ago.

In couple relationships, men or women who lodge in their mates this way avoid their feelings of disconnection—sadness, loneliness, vulnerability, uncertainty, and fear—by maintaining the seemingly infinite security of never having to stand separate on their own two feet. They love their Pretend Person. So they cannot, of course, love their real mate. Physical and verbal abusers make this mistake. As if to reaffirm their love of the Pretend Person, after an assault batterers may unabashedly say, "I loved her [or him] too much."

In an extreme case, when someone murders the person in whom they have anchored, the one in whom they have planted their Pretend Person, their connection is severed by their own hand. They have cut themselves adrift. Consequently, they often feel suicidal unless they can quickly find another person in whom to anchor. This is how powerful the Pretend Person is. It is rooted so deeply in the mind of the Pretender (as well as the body of the other) that the Pretender experiences it as a connection to reality itself.

Why do people approach others backwards, make up a Pretend Person, and anchor it in someone? Does this phenomenon have something to do with the experience of closeness?

Chapter XII

The Teddy Illusion

We may not know that it's there until we see its impact.

I n couple relationships, people who attempt to control their mate have created a Pretend Person whom they think *is* their mate. They relate to the Pretend Person that they mistake for their real mate. Let's take a look at how the Pretender creates, sees, and interacts with the Pretend Person. If we understand what is going on when someone makes up the other in a personal relationship, we will not only be better able to protect ourselves from anyone's attempt to control us, but also will better see what control is all about, even when it involves large groups.

The following drama, "The Teddy Illusion," shows just how someone might begin to "make up" a Pretend Person, and what happens in relationships when they do. Teddy starts out as a pretend friend, an imaginary teddy bear, and later Teddy is the main character.

An imaginary teddy bear provides the best example of how a Pretender develops and anchors a Pretend Person in someone, and shows how different a Pretend Person is from an authentic person. A teddy bear is inanimate, that is, quiet and totally compliant. This is just how the Pretender seems to expect the authentic person to be. Beginning in childhood, the Pretender unconsciously develops the Pretend Person like a child develops a pretend-friend teddy bear, and like a child who plugs every move and thought into his teddy bear making it "do" and "say" what he wants, the Pretender quite unconsciously tries to do the same thing. Only the Pretender is plugging the Pretend Person into an authentic person!

Teddy, like a real teddy bear, doesn't leave, is as comforting as one can imagine, and could be male or female, child or adult, or could even be split into a number of imaginary people. In the Pretender's earliest childhood, Teddy (Pretend Person) might begin as an imaginary, all-need-meeting parent and later be personified as a perfect mate.

In the following scenario, Teddy becomes a Pretend

Person—an imaginary mate that the Pretender anchors in a real person, and sees instead of that person.

The Teddy Illusion

I invite you to relax and imagine, if you will, that when very young you had an imaginary teddy bear. And you played with your imaginary teddy bear in the same way that children play with a real teddy bear.

Like playing house with dolls, imagine playing the roles of little Teddy *and* Teddy's friend, just as a child plays. The child's voice is high and even more childlike when talking with Teddy. "Hi, Teddy. Now you stay here, I'll be right back. Okay?"

"Okay," says Teddy in the same little voice.

With this picture in mind, please visualize having your own imaginary teddy bear right with you and imagine talking to Teddy and responding for Teddy with the same little voice.

The more you are able to put yourself into the imaginary world of the child playing "let's pretend," the more effective this scenario will be in revealing how some people establish an extension that like a tentacle reaches from one person into the other.

Are you ready?

ॐ ॐ ॐ

"Hey," you say to Imaginary Teddy Bear, "I'll be back later."

"Okay, bye," says Teddy, in the same little voice.

"Hi, I'm back."

"Oh! Hi, here I am," says Teddy.

You hug Teddy while you watch some cartoons on TV.

The next day, you say "Bye" as you go out the door. Teddy says, "Bye."

Days pass in much the same way. Sometimes you show Teddy things.

"Look what I made today."

And Teddy says, "Oh! You're really smart."

You have different things to tell Teddy, and Teddy knows just what to say.

Sometimes you just leave Teddy sitting around. But that's okay. Teddy's always there. Sometimes you grab Teddy and give a big hug. You're glad to have Teddy because no one else seems to care.

Most of the time you tell Teddy "Bye" when you leave, and Teddy never fails to say "Bye" back.

And Teddy always appreciates you. Teddy always thanks you for a taste of your candy and some of the good snacks you have.

Teddy is so nice to have around. You dream of Teddy and in some ways it almost seems that Teddy is alive.

Time passes.

"Hi, Teddy," you say.

"Hi," says Teddy.

"Bye," you say as you leave.

"Bye," says Teddy.

You dream of Teddy even more and Teddy becomes more and more real to you.

Then one day your dream Teddy is more than just a dream.

"Would you like some coffee?" asks Teddy.

Teddy moves around now, but as you look back it's hard to remember how it all came about. Anyway, this is great. You couldn't be happier. Teddy gets things done, agrees with you, of course, and thinks of things to do for you, even before you ask. So sometimes you give Teddy a list of things to do for you. You sure love Teddy.

You come and go as usual.

"I'll be back later," you say.

"Okay, bye," says Teddy in a familiar little voice.

"Hi, I'm back."

"Hi," says Teddy.

Time passes, and life continues quite the same. Teddy comes and goes, too, and gets money you can use and always is home for you. Sometimes Teddy talks about stuff but *it doesn't have anything to do with you,* so you just nod now and then. Sometimes you tell Teddy something about what you did at work and Teddy says something like "Oh, that's great. You're really smart."

You know Teddy wants what you want.

Each morning as usual you say, "Bye, I'll be back later." And Teddy says, "Okay, bye."

Each evening as usual you say, "Hi! I'm back."

And Teddy says, "Hi!"

The days go on and on much the same and you feel okay.

As time passes, once in a while Teddy says something that sounds strangely different, so you don't even nod. It's really just noise. *Nothing to do with what you're thinking.*

Then one morning you say "Bye!"

And in a very normal voice—one you've never heard before—Teddy says, "When will you be back?"

You're stunned! Your world is suddenly turned upside down. Nothing like this shattering experience ever happened before.

The Teddy you've always known is gone! Part of your mind wants to scream. *Where did my Teddy go?* Teddy has never acted like this! Teddy's so different! So suddenly separate. You feel almost annihilated. So alone. So shocked. It's as if Teddy's against you.

"What do you mean, 'When will I be back'?" you say, raging through clenched teeth, feeling attacked.

Everything seems to be falling apart. *All because of Teddy. How could Teddy do this?* Anger courses through you.

"Just what the hell are you questioning me for? All you do is question me!" you say. Beside yourself, you're barely able to think.

In the tiniest of voices, Teddy says, "I just wanted to know if there'd be time for me to stay for a meeting and still have dinner with you, or if you were getting home early."

Suddenly you hear Teddy's little voice. It sounds familiar.

"Well, why didn't you just say so! Damn it!"

"But that's all I needed to know—when you'd be home," says Teddy.

"Would you just quit going on and on. Always trying to be right," you say, as you go out the door.

Busy all day, you head for home that evening wanting nothing more than to relax and cuddle up with Teddy.

You come in as usual.

"Hi, Teddy!"

"Oh, hello," says Teddy, in a different voice.

"What the hell's wrong with you?" you say, tired

and exasperated and scared because Teddy sounds different. Not like Teddy at all.

In a pained way, Teddy says, "Well, I feel kind of sad. Are you angry with me about something?"

"I don't know where you get these ideas! Who've you been talking to?"

"I just want to know what you were angry about," says Teddy.

You feel an even greater rush of anger. "Nothing! I told you! Now will you just drop it? You never give up. I'm sick of your questions," you say.

Teddy stays quiet.

Everything is back to normal.

Next day, you say, "Bye, Teddy."

Teddy says "Bye" in a little voice.

You think, *Everything's okay.*

"Hi, Teddy," you say, as you come in that evening.

No voice greets you. You look around.

There's Teddy, sitting in the bedroom.

"What's the matter with you now?" you say.

"Nothing is the matter with me. I've just been thinking," says Teddy. "I think there's a problem in our relationship and I want you to go to a counselor with me about it."

"What the hell should I see a counselor for," you say, with disgust. Then angrily you say, "You're the one who's been acting strange. You've got a major psychological problem."

"I don't," says Teddy, sounding angry.

"Well, go see a counselor by yourself. You're the one who needs it. Look how you've been acting lately," you say as you walk out of the room.

A few days later, Teddy goes off to see a counselor.

You arrive home, saying, "Hi" as you come in.

"I want to ask you something," says Teddy.

"Well, what now? Just say it."

"The counselor says to ask you to come in with me," says Teddy, looking very still and staring straight ahead.

"What counselor?"

"The one I called, because I was feeling so sad, and I'm really mad too. This whole thing is so confusing," says Teddy.

"Why should I?"

"Because the counselor wants you to," says Teddy.

"Well if it'll straighten you out, then I guess I haven't any choice. When do we have to go?"

Teddy tells you. And on the appointment day you leave together. You're hoping Teddy will settle down if you just go once. You can't seem to make Teddy happy no matter how hard you try. You never even complain when Teddy doesn't get everything on the list done. And this is what you get for all your trouble. Just when the relationship is going great, Teddy has to start something.

At the appointment you tell the counselor how Teddy's been acting hostile lately, questioning you, seeming to have changed radically in the last year.

The counselor asks Teddy to try to understand how upset you've been and asks Teddy to try to be more accepting, to show more affection, to stop questioning you, and to be assertive.

The counselor asks you to be patient with Teddy and recommends a doctor who can give Teddy some antidepressants because Teddy seems especially sad.

Maybe it's a winter depression and Teddy needs

more sunlight, she says.

If that doesn't help, she knows a doctor who can tell if Teddy needs some hormones.

You're relieved that there's someone to help get Teddy back to normal.

Life goes on the same for the next couple of weeks.

"Hi, Teddy," you say, as you arrive home one day.

There is no answer. You look around and find Teddy in the bedroom packing a suitcase.

"What the hell are you doing?"

In a very tiny voice, Teddy says, "I'm leaving. Nothing has worked. I have to go."

"You're not going anywhere," you say. "Not after all I've done for you."

Suddenly Teddy snaps the suitcase shut, grabs it, and runs to the door. You chase Teddy. Furious. Suddenly you grab Teddy, all the while shouting as you push Teddy to the floor.

"I've had it with you! You're crazy! Even a therapist couldn't help you. You try that again and I'll have you committed," you say. You feel like jumping and pounding on Teddy, but you don't.

Secretly you hear a little voice inside saying, *I'm not going to play with you anymore. I'm going to find a nice, new Teddy.*

Teddy sits quietly in a corner.

Maybe Teddy got the message, you think. *Everything seems normal—as good as it did years ago. Teddy's stopped acting up.*

Next day, "Bye, Teddy," you say.

"Bye," says Teddy, very quickly.

As you head for home that evening you wonder why Teddy isn't any fun anymore.

You arrive home. Teddy is gone. For some reason you feel some part of you is gone too.

≀   ≀   ≀

This story is familiar to many people. They think it's about them.

"My Teddy was happy for me. I thought it meant we were of one mind. My mind. It never occurred to me to ask my Teddy what was wrong," said a client.

Another person, long separated from her husband, said she'd recently heard from him. He said he couldn't understand why she had left him and he wanted her to get back together with him. She told him she just couldn't do that.

Then she went on to tell me that when she had told him her reasons, he'd told her that she should have known he wasn't going to kill her.

"Kill you? What was he talking about?" I asked.

"When he had the knife to my throat, that's when he said I *should have known* he wasn't going to kill me."

One mind again!

"He is a little saner now," she said. "He stopped stalking me. I only had to move across town to escape his persecution. Look at the people who have to leave their country to escape it."

It is no wonder that the former husband believed she knew what he had in mind. He'd made her up. They were "so close." How could it be otherwise?

Just as if it were a human power, a psychic skill honed with exercise, some people pretend that they can cross your psychic boundary, look around, step out, and tell you what they've found there, "The trouble with you is _____," despite the fact that this is impossible.

When people are defined by someone with whom they are trying to relate, they feel psychically raped. In relationships we are vulnerable and open and therefore such assaults are quite devastating.

This is very different from an intuitive or sensitive person "reading" you by invitation. Your belief or disbelief in such a reading is your own business.

In everyday life, people who present reality backwards commonly mix up physical reality. For example, when someone says, "You made me _____," they are not only absolving themselves of all responsibility but also acting as if another party (you) were inside *them* and caused their behavior—as if this were within the natural order of things, founded in the reality of physical existence.

Although no one can actually be within another person and make them do what they do, or say what they say, some people pretend they can.

Similarly, a person who bullies another person may claim, in a backwards way, "It takes two," as if the "victim" had bullied the perpetrator.

Some people may even claim to reverse the past and present, pretending that their words in the present will change the past. For example, when a person acts violently against others and then says that they don't mistreat anyone, they make up the past and they make up themselves.

In the same way that a person makes up a Pretend Person, he or she may also make up a pretend world. In a pretend world, saying it is so makes it so.

Chapter XIII

The Spell

*Good people can fall under
the spell's influence.*

W hy do well-intentioned people—people who believe they're doing "what's right"—define others? What compels someone to break through another person's psychic boundary, disregarding it altogether? Isn't it enough just to be in charge of one's own reality—mind, body, and spirit?

If a person pretends to know someone else's inner world, aren't they under the influence of some illusion, something like a spell? Wouldn't they otherwise feel infantile? Embarrassed? Or at the very least silly? Wouldn't they stop as soon as they were reminded of what they were doing?

When people forge illusory connections to others, "making them up" as if they lived within them, the connections, although absurd, seem so very real to their makers, it is as if they are under a spell.

I would say that there is a spell, and the Teddy Illusion is part of it. I believe that possibly no one is completely free of the spell's influence at all times and in all circumstances. I also believe that one of our greatest desires is to be free from its illusions and that such freedom will come out of our curiosity, our burning desire to know and to understand.

In the following story we will look more closely at the possibility of a spell at work and how a person seemingly under its influence casts another person into a role not of their own choosing.

The Corn Story, Part I

At a farmer's market on a recent Saturday morning in a nearby town, I stood in line behind a well-dressed elderly couple waiting to buy corn. When their turn came I heard the woman ask for two dozen ears of corn. They were being sold at three ears for a dollar. She handed over two ten-dollar bills.

When she received her change, she expressed surprise

because it included one of the ten-dollar bills. "Wow! I didn't think I'd get this much back for twenty-four ears," she said, laughing. "Guess it's too early in the morning to figure it."

Suddenly everyone's attention was riveted on the man with her, as he shouted angrily, "She can't even count the goddamn change!"

The woman, seemingly as shocked by his roaring declaration as were the bystanders, was silent. But she seemed stunned.

As the couple left, the people in the line behind me began to talk about what the man had said. They expressed their shock and dismay. Someone said they thought he was ranting. Someone else said he was swearing. As I thought about the incident, I found it most significant that the husband (I did find out later that they were married) pretended that his wife couldn't count change and acted as if that "fact" appalled and infuriated him. Moreover, it seemed as if he were restricted in some way from finding out if what appalled him might *not* be true.

If he hadn't been restricted, wouldn't he have asked his wife in a private moment if she were having trouble counting change? If he thought she were, wouldn't he want to check it out? Wouldn't he feel sad and concerned for her? Wouldn't that be more humane behavior?

I think that what held him back from behaving rationally and from finding out the truth about his wife added to his fury. Whatever it was, it had a tremendous hold on him—so much so that it was as if he were under a spell. I wouldn't blame his behavior on a spell, nor excuse him for it, nor say that he was not responsible for it, but its influence was so great that it was *like* a spell.

The "spell" blinded the man to the fact that only his wife could know if and when she could count change, and to the fact that her knowledge of herself was within an *inaccessible* space. Her personal reality was unknowable. The man seemed to think that he knew his wife's inner world, but unless he checked it out—asked her—how could he?

Like the people in the previously mentioned stories, this man "had it backwards." He acted as if he could do the impossible—define his wife before she defined herself to him. I thought it even more amazing that he was enraged by his own fabrication.

I've seen that when people act in ignorance of what seems to be a spell, it becomes stronger. If they continue their backward approaches to the extreme, with nothing to stop them—no sign that says: "BACKWARDS: Wrong Way"—they fall more and more under the spell's influence and their behavior becomes increasingly bizarre. While some people have an inner "stop," a "red light" that halts extreme behavior, some people don't. And some run red lights.

The phenomenon of approaching people backwards can begin innocuously, but it can quickly become dangerous, not only to the people who are defined, but also to the people who do the defining. Has a spell affected their reason? Has something like a spell adversely impacted their ability to live satisfying, healthy lives? Let's keep our spotlight on this spell and see what we can discover.

The Corn Story, Part II

After buying a dozen ears of corn myself, I took them out to my car in the lot next to the market. A man, putting some bags in the trunk of a car parked next to mine, looked up and said, "Are you leaving now?"

"No," I said, with a slight question in my voice.

Sensitively, he noticed my tone and quickly explained himself. "I want to be sure you have enough room to back out and that I haven't parked too close."

"I've plenty of room. Thanks!" I said.

I recognized him then. He was the same man who had been taken over by rage (or possibly the spell) a few minutes before!

He seemed so different now. I wanted to be sure it was he. "Weren't you in the line buying corn?" I asked.

"My wife, the *war zone*, was," he said ferociously. Chameleon-like, he'd changed from a sensitive person into a growling one.

Stunned, I thought, *I've got to say something. He's just defined her again.*

"The people in the line are talking about what they heard you say about your wife," I said evenly

His mouth actually dropped open. He said nothing.

My statement had invited him to reflect upon his behavior.

I went back to finish my shopping. Maybe, just for a moment, he saw himself mirrored in the eyes of another.

I don't know if I shattered his illusions and broke the spell he seemed to be under. But a spell, in fact, is a way to describe a collection of illusions, including the Teddy Illusion. The word "spell" gives the collection of illusions a name so that we can begin to talk about them. The coming chapters will reveal the illusions, the depth of the spell, and the compelling force behind it.

The people with backwards approaches in the stories "Smile," "You Read Too Much," and "The Corn Story" acted foolishly. Whether harmlessly or harmfully, in all cases they seemed to be unaware of the absurdity of their own behavior and unconscious of their own motives. Instead, they seemed convinced of their "rightness."

Automatically, often harmlessly, such phrases as, "Smile, it's a nice day" or "You read too much" spatter us like rain, not necessarily seeping in, nor dampening our spirit, but deserving of our awareness. If we don't heed this rain, it can become a torrent. Our spirit, like fire, can be dampened. It *can* die down. When people tell us how we *are*, how we *do*, or what we *should* do, they practice a dangerous kind of sorcery.

Even when you don't believe another person's definition of you, their disregard of your individuality can disturb your well-being.

A couple came to me for a consultation. Curt and Dora both seemed to want a happy relationship, but every now and then "something happened." In this case, Dora described one particular thing Curt had said that really bothered her. Curt couldn't remember the incident. But Dora insisted she knew it had happened. Curt said it hadn't. At this point I didn't know whom to believe.

Usually, when someone is very upset over an incident and describes in detail what is bothering them and why they have felt hurt, as Dora did, some kind of assault has actually taken place.

Although Curt could have been connected in a backwards way to Dora, I wasn't sure. Then Curt turned to me and said, "After couple's counseling, we usually leave hating each other." I saw the stricken look on Dora's face. It wasn't his casualness that struck her. It was that he said she'd felt hate towards him *as if he were within her* and knew her feelings.

As it turned out, she hadn't felt hate or anything like it. She had come to my office out of pain, frustration, and confusion. She wanted to love and be loved. But before she could have a loving relationship with Curt, Curt would have to see her as a separate person.

As if he were beside himself and *in* Dora, Curt had defined her inner reality, obliterating it and replacing it with his version, all in an effort to make light conversation about their situation. And he didn't see her pain.

Dora had long struggled to get him to see what he was doing. She hadn't lost her spirit. It was simply draining from her through the open wounds of such invasions. And no one had noticed, least of all her husband.

Unless we know about the spell, people under its influence might convince us of their "rightness" and we may find ourselves under *their* influence. If we are under their influence, we can lose not only knowledge of ourselves but also our spirit. The following tale shows how this can happen.

A Tale of Two Women

Once upon a time there was a woman who felt the amazing grace of a transcendent moment filled with extraordinary peace and joy.

She recalled a time in her childhood when her mother had reminded her, "The kingdom of heaven is within." These words took on a meaning and depth she had never known before and from time to time, when she felt the need, she recalled her transcendent experience and again felt renewed and supported.

A second woman, like the first, felt the special grace of a transcendent moment filled with extraordinary peace and joy. After a time she too felt a need for renewal and support. As was her custom, she went to those who said that they were the authorities in all matters of the spirit. The authorities then told her that they held the key to the kingdom she sought.

She said, "Okay."

She did not doubt them. They did not doubt themselves. But she had given up her key. Because she believed them, she fell under their influence and ultimately under their control.

Clearly, it is not only day-to-day training that can keep us from our inner knowing, but also our beliefs. If we believe that others are the authority on our inner experience, we doubt ourselves and become subject to others' definitions of us and subject to their control of us.

Most people who are under the influence of the spell say that they do not intend to exert control over anyone. But what compels oppressive behavior?

Although it has been said that people who try to control other people suffer from low self-esteem, this is not *necessarily* true of people with oppressive behaviors. Even those who do have low self-esteem have the option of choosing another way to raise it. Aren't there many ways to feel better about oneself? Why not make a sale, paint a picture, clean out the garage, work as a volunteer, learn something new? The sense of accomplishment derived from such endeavors brings satisfaction and goes a long way toward tempering, even eradicating, negative feelings about oneself. Why attempt to control others instead?

Clearly, the issue of self-esteem is not the primary cause of oppressive behavior. People don't try to control others just because they don't feel good about themselves. Rather, they are under the spell, constrained by a whole collection of illusions. These illusions are signs of the spell because they are in effect wherever the spell is at work. We've already seen one: the Teddy Illusion. Here are some more examples of illusions that comprise the spell.

Illusions of the Spell

People who are under the spell are acting under one or more of the following illusions:

- They can actually define another person or group.
- Their definition of another person or group is true.
- Another person or group is responsible for their actions.
- Another person or group may not have their own separate opinion.
- Another person or group causes their behavior.

Also, before they have concrete evidence or have been informed by the person or group in question, they are under the illusion that they know something about the other, i.e., what the other . . .

- thinks
- is trying to do
- has done
- means
- should do
- should be

- wants
- needs
- feels
- intends
- did
- expects

Or, they think they know that the other person or group is wrong.

People who are under the spell are also sure that:

- their behavior is not odd, senseless, or harmful
- they do not cross a psychic boundary
- they are right
- they are not under any illusions
- they are not playing "let's pretend"
- they are independent and self-reliant
- [and in some cases] God has chosen their side

These illusions, reinforced by culture and family, lead some people to believe that they "know" about others, can interpret their motives and feelings, and can tell them what is "wrong" with them or what they should and should not do.

In a healthy relationship a misunderstanding can occur at any time. One simply asks for clarification: "Do you mean . . . ?" or states what is true for them, and that is accepted. But if someone is connected to you backwards, they may make up something about you, fabricating it on the pretext discussed earlier: that they have access to your personal reality and know more about you than you know about yourself. This is surely spellbound behavior, when even our most common greetings, "How are you?" and "How do you do?" acknowledge that our personal reality is our own. I *don't* know how you are, *nor* do I know how you do.

It is one thing to be under the influence of the spell and quite another to be under the influence of people who are under the influence of the spell. People who are unknowingly under the influence of people who are under the influence of the spell are likely to have one or more of the following illusions:

- It is reasonable for one human being to define another human being.
- They are stuck with another person's definition of them.
- They do not have the right to their own opinions.
- They can earn love and acceptance by abdicating to another person.
- They are "successful" if they fulfill another person's vision, even when it does not in any way support their own.
- They must have permission to act in matters that are their own business.

The stories in the previous chapters demonstrate the many ways that people approach others backwards and even attempt to make backwards connections. We've seen the absurdity as well as the consequences of these behaviors, and we've noticed how they seem to be overlooked or not understood because the spell appears to be at work in many people's lives. Now, let's look beyond the spell into the Control Connection itself.

Chapter XIV

The Control Connection

*The Control Connection
substitutes for
connection to self.*

T o control is to act to effect an outcome, generally by means of restraint, physical or verbal, with regard to self, others, or the world around one.

There are two kinds of control. One is the nurturing control that we have over ourselves, our lives, and those entrusted to our care. The other is oppressive control.

Nurturing control supports one's own and others' freedom to be themselves, while oppressive control does just the opposite. Most people exercise nurturing control throughout their lives by the choices they make and the actions they take to ensure their own and others' sustenance and survival: to put off immediate gratification for a future good; to manage their resources—money, time, space, and environment; to pursue their work and their relationships; and to care for their children and their families. In other words, to direct their lives, but not at the expense of another.

When Pretenders connect backwards, anchor in someone, and then attempt to keep their Pretend Person alive and well and exactly as they want him or her to be, they attempt to control the individual in whom they've anchored. Some people are aware of their behavior. Some are not. Some comprehend the likely outcome. Most do not.

If Pretenders don't get out from under the influence of the spell, they launch even greater assaults, especially if their definition of the other is not accepted, that is, they can't make "Teddy," their pretend person, appear. In this way Pretenders exert increasingly oppressive behavior. In relationships, while they may believe that they are only getting closer (bringing Teddy to life, so to speak), they are, in fact, aligning with the forces of oppression.

On one side, the person defined by the Pretender usually experiences this behavior as restrictive, oppressive, or as an attempt by the Pretender to control him or her. But if the person defined is very young or very naive, he or she may be unable to recognize the control tactic and may simply agree with the Pretender, taking in the Pretender's definiton as truth. On the other side, the Pretender is attempting to gain or experience an ongoing kind of connection—a feeling of closeness. Hence, I call this way of connecting to another person a *Control Connection.*

Although people may connect in a backwards way to anyone—for instance, to a celebrity whom they've never met—it is only when they actually try to get that person to be their Pretend Person that they attempt to control him or her. Then their backwards connection becomes a Control Connection.

The Control Connection reflects a *way of being in the world*—a backwards (outside-in) way of orienting toward one or more people that is so ineffectual and dangerous that it catapults us toward a world that is becoming ever more violent.

Control connections are established by people who are beside themselves, who need to get a grip, not on something tangible, but *within* someone else in order to feel connected, to feel close or, especially where groups are concerned, to feel right.

In adult familial or couple relationships, people who are or have been connected to in this backwards way almost always feel alone, unaccepted, and unknown, even though they may not know why they feel this way. If their attempts to be seen and heard are futile, eventually they may experience anxiety, depression, panic attacks, eating disorders, post-traumatic stress disorders, or other emotional difficulties. Physically, the symptoms are exhaustion and a compromised immune system with stress-related illnesses including exhaustion, digestive disorders, chronic fatigue, even cancer.

Notes from a conversation with a client:

She was too sick to leave. Highly stressed. Married to a man who attempted to control everything about her. She had no access to money. Once when she asked him, "What would make you happy?" he told her "That you have no friends, talk to no one, and just wait all day for me to come home." [a perfect Teddy]

Since a Control Connection is a backwards connection, it is the exact opposite of a true connection. It is a sick substitute for the real thing. It is also something more than projection as described in psychological literature. It is a backwards way of experiencing one's connection to reality itself.

In order to understand the backwards quality of a Control Connection, let's first look at a healthy connection between two people. A healthy connection is one that recognizes the individuality of the other. As two people communicate verbally as well as with their tone of voice, facial expressions, and body language, they each respond appropriately to what they hear and see. For instance, hearing good news one might say, "Oh, that's great." Seeing sadness: "Is something bothering you?" "Do you want to talk about it?" They clarify any ambiguity: "Do you mean this?" When they see and hear each other, they can establish an empathetic connection.

But when people establish a Control Connection, it is quite the *opposite*. I invite you to visualize such a connection. Imagine saying to a friend, "Hi, Joe. How are you doing?" But your communication never reaches Joe. In fact, Joe says, "What do you mean 'How am I doing?' You know goddamn well how I'm doing."

This is what happens when someone "cannot" hear you. Instead of your "signals" reaching them and their responding to you, a wall seems to stand between you, blocking your communication. The wall is a Pretend Person. Joe's Pretend Person just wouldn't say "How are you doing?"; Pretend Person already knows how Joe's doing, *of course*.

If you were in a familial relationship with Joe, would you try to explain to Joe that you really didn't know how he was doing? Very commonly people in familial or work relationships do try to explain.

I invite you to imagine that a Pretender *lives* within you via a Pretend Person, so that the Pretender *knows* what you should say, do, think, etc. The Pretender also *knows* that *you* know what they mean and how they feel without being told! Imagine how irritated or angry the Pretender feels when you don't say or do what he or she wants. Encounters with Pretenders can be devastating and seemingly inexplicable.

It is all like a dream, possibly a nightmare. Pretend Person is, in every sense of the word, a "dream" person.

Once Pretenders have planted a Pretend Person in someone, they believe that they are rational when they say, for instance, "You knew what I meant," or "You know how I feel." They have mistaken you for their Pretend Person—a dream person who would know what they meant or how they feel.

Quite commonly, people who mysteriously anchor within you this way will unwittingly reveal that they have, in fact, done so. Most often they reveal this backwards connection when they define you. For example, after looking around here at your nervous system I can tell that you're made wrong: "You're too sensitive," voiced with real conviction, because the dream person would never have complained.

In another example, when a person says, "You don't know what you're talking about," it is as if they were saying, "After looking around here in your mind I can tell you that your opinion is formed wrong." The dream person would never have had that opinion.

Most people feel confused, sad, or outraged when they are so invaded. In other instances such intrusions seem silly, like nonsense. In any case, resisting these intrusions is spell-breaking. But if the spell is *not* broken, Pretenders feel anything from irritation to rage and will believe themselves threatened or attacked. Only if the spell is truly broken will the Pretender awaken.

When Pretenders define groups, they experience an intensified form of the Control Connection. We'll explore this connection later when we navigate the territory of individual-to-group and group-to-group connections.

Chapter XV

The Controller
and the Witness

---

*It wasn't that he wanted
to control her, he said. It was
that he wanted to have the
dream person be alive.*

With the understanding that a person is not his or her behavior, I describe the person who establishes and attempts to maintain a Control Connection as *Spellbound* and refer to him or her as the *Controller.*

In many couple relationships there are Pretenders and Controllers. Pretenders make up a pretend or dream person, pick out a body, and when they feel secure, anchor their dream person in it; that is, they act as if the dream person has replaced the real person. Controllers are Pretenders who go one step further. They will try to maintain the dream person by any means necessary, by fighting, or ignoring all ideas, opinions, and so forth expressed by the *real* person.

Occasionally an exception occurs. In this exception, instead of fighting or ignoring his or her partner's ideas or accomplishments, the Controller does the opposite. The Controller pretends the partner's ideas and opinions are his or her own.

For instance, a person says or does something that the Controller wishes he or she had said or done. The Controller then pretends to have said or done it, taking credit for the other's achievements and talents. In another example, the boss regularly asks an employee for his opinions regarding an important topic to be discussed at an upcoming meeting. Shortly after, the boss presents the ideas at the meeting as if they were his or her own. Whether Controllers fight others' ideas and opinions or claim them as their own, they do not respect their source.

Controllers don't empathize with the "other," because to do so would mean letting go of the dream person. If they let go of their dream person, where would they be? Disconnected. Such a conscious act would take courage.

Some people are trained to tolerate control, to "make their relationship work." If you had this training, it is important to know that the dream person is a mirage changing from moment to moment. It cannot be embraced by even the most compliant person. And it is not safe to do so. Controllers can continue to the extreme. Some Controllers make up pretend groups or even a pretend world. For them, the dream person of their relationship is only the beginning.

On the other hand, once they are anchored in someone, some Controllers appear to be respectful of most people. Not surprisingly, they may be described as kind, thoughtful, even charming by those with whom they have not established a Control Connection. Indeed they see themselves in this positive light. Some even think of themselves as wonderful because they have built their identity from the outside in, according to their chosen "wonderful" model.

Most of us only rarely fall under the influence of the spell, because we are beside ourselves only under rare circumstances—for instance, when jolted from ourselves by traumatic events. Controllers, however, have adopted a "beside-themselves" lifestyle.

The Witness

With the understanding that a person is not his or her behavior, I describe the person who is defined by the Controller as the *Witness*. When Witnesses resist Controllers they become *Spellbreakers*. Some groups act collectively as a Witness or a Spellbreaker.

Often, when Witnesses are treated oddly or badly, they don't understand what they are witnessing. They experience the Controller as oppressive, unaccepting, hard to understand, erratic, and/or dangerous. Of course, Controllers can be all of these, but even when Witnesses know that they are in the presence of a Controller, they usually do not know that the Controller is *actually attempting to maintain an illusory connection via a Pretend Person*. Generally speaking, the Controller doesn't know it either.

In the workplace, control connections jeopardize the health and well-being of employees. A saleswoman told me that her boss repeatedly said, "You aren't trying." But she was trying to do a good job and, in fact, she was doing it very well. She didn't realize that her boss was defining her intentions *before* he asked her what they were, and that he was actually trying to get her to conform to his pretend person (possibly a billion-dollar dream saleswoman). She worked double time to prove she really was trying. Soon she felt burned out and left her job. Her employer lost an outstanding employee.

Control Connections in familial relationships are truly devastating. Once the Controller creates a pretend partner, child, etc., he or she can neither hear nor see the real person and so defines him or her in myriad ways. Controllers will indulge in this behavior whenever they feel that their Pretend Person (their Teddy) is not there for them.

Since a Pretend Person originates with the Pretender and is in the Pretender's mind, it is felt to be a *part* of the Pretender. For example, in the Teddy Illusion, the Pretender feels intimately connected to Pretend Person, Teddy, and close, because, like a dream, Pretend Person is a part of him or her—a figment of his or her imagination. As a general rule, in familial relationships, the moment that the Pretender anchors in the other, *mistaking* the other for the Pretend Person, he or she becomes a Controller and feels closer than ever before.

Mistaking the other for an illusory person explains a strange paradox: that some people in couple or parent/child relationships truly believe that they *love* the other while they act in hurtful, alienating, or even hateful ways, trying to change a real person into an illusory one.

A man described this paradoxical behavior: "I love her more than anyone on planet Earth. She is my soul mate. And I destroyed her."

Generally, when someone is defined or treated with hostility there are: (1) a Pretend Person—the Teddy Illusion, (2) a Pretender—the person who pretends, (3) an authentic person—the Witness, (4) a Controller—the person who defines the Witness, and (5) a Spellbreaker who tries to be seen and heard.

In Betty's story, the Pretend Person was the "daughter-who-likes-chocolate-walnut-best." The Pretender was Betty. Betty became the Controller by defining Suzy. The Witness was Suzy. When Suzy tried to be seen and heard and refused to accept her mother's definition of her, she became a Spellbreaker.

Parents who make up a pretend child will define their own child when he or she doesn't act like their pretend child.

"You're hopeless," was how some fathers defined their sons in the past and maybe still do, thinking, *because you will not do things my way—be my pretend son*. And "You're looking for trouble," was how some mothers defined their daughters, and maybe still do, thinking, *because you will not do things my way—be my pretend daughter*.

In almost all cases, Controllers are amazingly unconscious of their behavior and their real motives. By unconscious I mean that they act without awareness. For instance, just as a person at any given moment may be unaware of how their back feels against a chair until their attention is drawn to it, Controllers are unaware of their behavior until their attention is directed to it. But it is not a simple problem of inattention—they fight awareness with great determination. They appear to be Spellbound.

Of all the people I've talked with who have established a Control Connection, whether to their mate, child, coworker, employee, boss, or a group, none started their day saying to him- or herself, "I'm going to control _____!" or, "I am going to pretend that this person or this group is _____!" Generally, the last thing that Controllers think of themselves is that they are playing "let's pretend" or, that they are attempting to control anyone.

If Controllers don't have a conscious intention to control someone or some group, what are they doing? What's happening? *They are reacting to perceived threats to their Control Connection.*

We have now encountered another strange paradox. Even though Controllers are almost constantly fighting to maintain their Control Connection, they do not realize that they have even established one. This is because they are, in fact, Spellbound.

The Spellbound

Let's take a look at some examples of Spellbound behavior. A Witness said, "I don't like to cook"; the Controller said, "Oh, that's not true. Everybody liked your pilaf at the party." (Pretend Person likes to cook.)

A Witness said, "I'm really looking forward to my trip"; the Controller said, "You don't like to be around me." (Pretend Person would never enjoy being away.)

A Witness said, "I don't want to continue dating you because I have very different values from some you've expressed"; the Controller said, "You are afraid of intimacy." (Teddy doesn't have different values.)

In none of these cases do the Controllers hear the Witnesses and respond to the communication. Instead, the

Controllers continue to make up something about the Witnesses, whose individuality remains unrecognized, as if their real selves are nonexistent.

In couple relationships, in which we hold hands as partners on the path of life, all partnership dissolves when a Control Connection is forged. Sometimes the Controller gets the *opposite* of what he or she intended, an empty hand.

A man told me that just seeing his wife sometimes "made" him feel irritable. But he had no idea why. If we look at his relationship in terms of our model, we can see that as time passes he might find it increasingly difficult to keep pretending—to maintain his Pretend Person. His wife might grow to be more expressive of her individuality, therefore less Teddy-like. Taking into account the objective of his oppressive behavior, to preserve his Control Connection, it is not surprising that he would feel increasingly thwarted and that he would become ever more oppressive. To the Controller, attempting to exert control is tantamount to working on the relationship, getting closer!

Generally, Controllers do all they can to preserve their Control Connection, while Witnesses do all they can to escape this extreme oppression. When Witnesses struggle to be seen and heard over many years, they become exhausted and can have little strength to escape.

In cases such as these, Controllers are shocked if the relationship ends. They not only don't know that they are pretending, they don't know that their ignorance predisposes them to mind-boggling behaviors. Their idea of themselves as "wonderful" blinds them to the impact of their behavior— reactions to, and defenses against, all threats to their illusory connection. They are difficult to deal with at best. They are terrifying and life-threatening at worst.

Controllers do not need to be forever Spellbound. They

can, themselves, break their Control Connections and, as we will see later on our journey, there are a growing number of possibilities that the spell itself can be broken. There are many more Spellbreakers in the world than there were even a few years ago. Many people see the nonsense for what it is. And they are learning more all the time. Already, many formerly Spellbound people have so agilely evaded the influence of the spell that they have contributed to the breaking of it.

Part II

We have come to a milestone in our journey of exploration through the maze of senseless behaviors woven into our world. We've seen how Controllers, under the influence of the spell, relate to self and others, how they create a Pretend Person, take up residence within someone, and become ever more oppressive, trying to control more frequently and intensely.

In the next section we will see why people who attempt to control others live with increasing anxiety and fear. Most of us have heard that people who try to control others do so out of fear. But just what exactly are they afraid of?

Chapter XVI

Plugged In and Powerless

The spell serves one primary purpose: to cloak Control Connections in a mantle of rationality.

In long-term relationships, the Control Connection is like a parasitic attachment. As we have seen, the Controller is anchored within the Witness by means of Pretend Person, protected, feeling close, and "being plugged in." On the other side, the Witness suffers the devastating experience of being shunned, unseen, unheard, and, in the eyes of the Controller, even nonexistent.

This leads us to another strange paradox. While the Controller seems quite powerful, overbearing, even frightening to the Witness, in relation to the Witness the Controller usually feels just the opposite: powerless.

I first came upon this strange paradox when I talked with Controllers who said that they felt attacked when their partners asked them to stop defining them.

For instance, when a Controller hears a plea such as, "Please don't talk to me like that," the Controller will usually say something like, "I don't need to be attacked like that," or, incredibly, "You're trying to control me." or, "I don't know why you have to start a fight just when everything's going fine."

As I discussed the concepts of separateness and individuality with Controllers, I discovered that when people are in control mode, i.e., are trying to control someone, they feel *plugged in and powerless*.

Why? Because they live in ever-present peril. If the Witness acts in an unanticipated, unscripted, spontaneous way, the Witness is a Spellbreaker. At *any moment a Witness may say or do something that threatens to dislodge the Controller—break the connection.* The Controller is then unanchored, disconnected from the Witness, alone.

This explains another strange paradox. Controllers usually see Witnesses as all-powerful, able to render the most horrendous of fates: disconnection. When the illusion of Pretend Person (Teddy) is lost or displaced by a real person, it is as if the tentacle trespassing the Witness's psychic boundary is damaged or *severed*. When this occurs, the Controller feels attacked, and, not knowing about the spell, the Controller is left with a terrible feeling of powerlessness.

Imagine being connected to nothing. A Controller explained what this would be like for him. He said that as he imagined seeing his wife as a separate person, he felt adrift, as if he were in outer space. He said that he was beginning to feel not just anxiety but panic. It is no wonder he felt this way. Being separate from his wife felt like being outside of reality as he knew it. No one could live adrift in outer space, but, I assured him, the sense of being adrift was a feeling, not a fact, and so would not kill him.

Pondering this case, I wondered what it would be like for a Controller to hear from a Witness, not Teddy's question, "When will you be back?" but something seemingly far worse: "I don't want to have dinner with you." Would this feel like a death threat?

At this point in our journey, it looks like the precarious position in which Controllers find themselves is in full view. They are utterly dependent upon their ability to keep someone or some group "made up." This is how they feel connected.

The man in "The Corn Story" is an example. He was enraged when his wife was uncertain about the amount of money she received in change. His rage was toward her authentic self. After all, she acted spontaneously, unexpectedly, certainly not like Teddy. Teddy would know.

Let's explore the territory he and other Controllers inhabit—the territory of the "plugged in and powerless."

People who act against us, who are plugged in and feeling powerless at the very moment that they act, don't think that they are accountable for their actions, because they are reacting to the threat of separateness, which is, of course the feeling of being beside themselves. Even as they deny their wrong doing, "I don't know what you're talking about," they are *most crucially denying the separateness of the other*.

A man said that all the time he was in jail for attacking his wife, he thought about how he would get even with her for his situation, as if he was serving time for her deeds and not his own. This is backwards, and typical of most batterers' thinking. Batterers are connected backwards to their partners. They have established a Control Connection.

Since Controllers don't feel separate, they are certain that the person they act against is responsible for their behavior: "You made me do it" or "I did it because you _____." By denying their separateness, they give away their own autonomy, pretend that they have *no* choice, and blame others for their behavior. And, most crucially, they give testimony to their condition: that of being plugged in and powerless. They fear separateness more than their loss of the freedom to choose. In effect, they define *themselves* as powerless. And, since they do not recognize the Witness's individuality, indeed, personhood, they do not recognize the effects of their behavior.

Although people who indulge in oppressive behaviors may apologize in order to avoid the consequences of their hurtful actions, rarely have I seen them deeply moved by the other's pain. In close relationships, some are able to cry for themselves. Rarely can they cry for the other. Only when the spell is broken is this possible.

A man who had indulged in oppressive behaviors and was committed to understanding and ending them shared the following results of an effort he made to understand his own feelings. I had invited him to imagine that his wife had a good idea about something that was quite different from any he'd come up with. Wonderfully articulate, he told me:

I hope that the following is as useful to you as it was to me.

As I followed the exercise you told me about, the first thing I noticed is that I was feeling fear and insecurity that my wife was "moving away" in having an idea that was not "my" idea, meaning the genesis of the concept was not from me.

It was very revelational: It was like my wife and I are in what's like a big soap "bubble," only firmer. The "bubble" is my reality. She has "freedom" as long as she stays in the "bubble." There is room to move about so the illusion of freedom seems real to her. But, when she expresses an idea, it's like she is stepping out of MY bubble and stepping into her own. But I do not want her out there. I fear being alone with me. I fear being with my feelings.

I try to pull her back into my "bubble" or WORSE injure her so she can never leave or WORSE yet, disorient her so she can never find her way out. That is the nature of my controlling moves. They tell her that she really DOESN'T want to move out of my "bubble" because it is not safe out of it.

Really, outside my bubble where I'm not in control is actually safer for her. The fact is that if she moves out of the "bubble" I do not feel safe, so I panic and try to keep her in my "bubble."

When she says "stop," I am instantly aware of being alone in the "bubble" and then I try to pull her back in. I know I have to let go and face the pain.

The pain has been there in the "bubble" the whole time, but as long as I am occupied with keeping my partner in my "bubble" I do not feel it or face it.

Right now, I'm thinking that the only way I can be

whole is for her to leave. For me to be alone and face the pain and grow.

Notice how he says, "The 'bubble' is my reality." Hence it is a mental construct. This suggests that if his wife is in his bubble, his wife is held in his mind as a Pretend Person (Teddy). To him, she and Pretend Person are "one." It is only when his wife appears separate, in her own "bubble" that he takes action to get her back in his "bubble," to stop her from showing signs of separateness. This is when he becomes a Controller.

As we continue our exploration, we confront yet another strange paradox. Generally speaking, Controllers *see* themselves as strong, independent, and in need of no one. Indeed they are usually seen by others in this light, but they battle feelings of powerlessness. They are extremely dependent upon the "other" because of their overriding fear of being disconnected. This fear is so great that their attempts to control the "other" are first and foremost designed to avoid being disconnected, and thus beside themselves once again.

One way Controllers respond to the loss of a mate, is to try to establish a new Control Connection within another candidate as quickly as possible. And still other Controllers deny the loss of their "walking, talking Pretend Person," by stalking the body, that is, the person who has left them, while still feeling connected to it, via their Pretend Person.

Since Controllers usually experience their Control Connection as a connection to reality itself, a threat to their Control Connection does, indeed, seem like a death threat, a cause for panic.

Disconnection is so terrifying to extreme Controllers that in certain instances they will kill a Witness to prevent the Witness from disconnecting, that is, leaving. When the deadly deed is done, they have made their greatest fear come true—in a final and physical way, they have, in fact, brought about the dreaded experience of disconnection. They often feel suicidal and some are so afflicted that they kill themselves. This is a common homicide/suicide scenario.

With a seemingly live Pretend Person (Teddy) by their side, Controllers have the safety and security of writing the script of Pretend Person's life—all in accordance with their own desires. They give orders and feel justifiably angry if their directions aren't followed and justifiably affronted, even enraged, if their mate shows a sign of separateness. They "naturally" define their partner, and "know" that their partner knows what they want and how they feel. Their feeling of being beside themselves dissolves into being connected within someone else. This way of connecting is a *way of being. It is almost as powerful as a connection to one's self.*

Controllers do not know about their own Pretend Person, nor do they understand the Control Connection and its being a substitute for actual human connection, nor do they even realize from whence their fear comes. In a strange and paradoxical way, their fear of disconnection is hidden from them by the Control Connection itself.

Intimacy is often a problem in couple relationships. One person wants intimacy. The other avoids it. Now we see a new way to look at the problem of *no* intimacy in what is meant to be an intimate relationship. Controllers fear intimacy because intimacy requires hearing and seeing one's mate for who she or he is. Intimacy severs the Control Connection.

Attempting intimacy, some Controllers have begun to face their fear of disconnection with true courage.

During a phone consultation, I suggested to the caller that he try a carefully constructed exercise involving the practice of nurturing communication. We discussed the details. It involved having a planned meeting with his wife, taping his words with his own recorder, and reviewing the conversation.

"I have one concern," he said beforehand.

"What's that?" I asked, wondering if he felt uncomfortable recording his words.

"How will I handle my anxiety if I actually do sit across from her and listen to her as if she *really* were a separate person?"

I acknowledged the impact of anxiety and how it was a telling sign of the fear of separateness. I told him that deep breathing helps and that I had yet to hear of someone dying of anxiety, and then I described the anxiety a person might feel who, no matter how they tried, could not be heard. He was able to understand that to relate to each other, two people need to perceive each other as separate individuals.

He thought about this, then said, "My anxiety is nothing compared to having *no* relationship."

Another man who had spent some time working on understanding his behavior, realized that he had created a dream woman and anchored it in his wife. He described how he had done this, and how he felt about giving up his Pretend Person.

"I blew her up like a balloon doll with my thoughts. Never really heard or saw her. Always told her how things were."

I was amazed that he saw himself so clearly. I had told him of the Teddy Illusion and had asked him if his mental picture of her (his Teddy) would have helped or hindered his actually hearing her.

He immediately said that it had gotten in the way and that he finally understood what had happened. Then he said something that told me quite dramatically that he did understand.

"Do you know what is really scary? That when I go home today I'll be seeing her for the first time. And I don't even know who she is!"

As we talked he realized that he had felt it necessary to ignore his wife because her authentic self threatened his *idea* of her—a dream woman whom until then he had actually thought *was* her.

Like many Controllers, he hadn't realized that he had not related to his wife. He'd thought they were close and that she was happy but he had, instead, spent many years close to, and enamored of, a dream woman. All the while his wife felt more and more estranged, alone, unheard, and unseen. *An authentic person cannot exist simultaneously with a Pretend Person in the mind of a Pretender.*

This explains a strange paradox: A Witness may tell of being severely abused by a mate and yet the very same mate will show every sign of admiring, even adoring, the protesting partner.

A young man, who had found himself attempting to control his partner, said that when he thought about seeing his girlfriend as separate from him, thought about hearing her and responding to her, he felt "pure panic."

As he imagined giving up his Pretend Person, he said that he felt that he would become nonexistent, "dissolved," as if he were "disconnected from planet Earth itself."

Who can survive being disconnected from reality—beyond the Earth and its nurturing atmosphere? Is there a way to survive the threat of disconnection? We'll find out later when we explore "Breaking the Spell."

People who forge Control Connections don't usually see themselves as controlling or oppressive. In familial relationships they usually believe that they love the person whom they are with.

A case in point: A client, typical of many, said, "When my wife handed me divorce papers, I felt like I'd been hit in the back with a sledgehammer. It was so unexpected and such a blow."

As the consultation continued, he told me that she did say there were things that bothered her, that she'd protested his statements, that she wished he wouldn't say and do certain things, that she'd asked him to stop, that she'd said she didn't want to live like this.

"So why were you surprised?" I asked.

"I couldn't hear her," he said.

In familial relationships, Pretend Person seems so real to Controllers, such a part of them and so intimately connected to them, that they do think of this strange closeness as love. But Control Connections only keep Controllers from becoming aware of what they're missing, real closeness.

Another important reason that Controllers don't recognize their dependency on Control Connections is that since they have made themselves up from the *out*side in, they are *already* living as if their personal reality were outside themselves, so connecting outside of themselves and in someone else seems normal.

Clearly, if people fear losing their "way of being" on planet Earth, that is, the anchor that makes it and them "real," they would be on the lookout for any threats to their connection. Confirmed Controllers, fearing disconnection, watch for and react immediately to signs of separateness.

Chapter XVII

Signs of Separateness

To the Controller, love is not wishing a partner the power and strength of their own personal reality, because that personal reality is a sign of separateness.

In familial relationships, it is the Witness's individuality itself that disturbs the Control Connection and threatens to break the spell. Any expression of individuality—a different opinion, for example—is also a sign of separateness and so is potentially spellbreaking.

In a healthy relationship, if one person finds ripe strawberries to be sweeter than ripe apricots and the other person experiences ripe apricots as sweeter than ripe strawberries, both persons may find this interesting or inconsequential, or even enhancing of their knowledge of each other, bringing them a bit closer together.

The Controller feels just the opposite—threatened, attacked, rejected—because "Teddy" isn't there. A *person* has taken Teddy's place, a person who doesn't have Teddy's tastes. Controllers react instantly to such displacement, *as if they themselves were being displaced.*

The fear of separateness underlies many acts of violence. For instance, an imprisoned Tibetan nun was reported to have been beaten up while in prison, and of dying from her injuries, for singing nationalist songs. Her separate opinions and feelings, even expressed in song, were so terrifying to her captors that they killed her.

These extremists may seem to be "crazy people." But I wonder if there is a Controller anywhere who has not felt threatened by a different opinion from a person he or she connected to backwards?

Usually Controllers are startled by specific signs of separateness. The signs are totally unexpected because the spell is so deep that the Controller doesn't realize an authentic person is "there." Or conversely, the Controller believes Pretend Person *is* the real person.

A different opinion is just one of many signs of separateness. Other signs of separateness can be the authentic expression of the following:

- New ideas
- Requests
- Thoughts
- Suggestions
- Questions
- Spontaneous expressions
- Style
- Insights
- Beliefs
- Misgivings
- Objections
- Apprehension

There are many more signs of separateness, including body language, independent actions, and so forth.

A 1996 study of 846 women on welfare in the United States reveals that forty percent were facing active oppression by mates who were trying to prevent them from gainful employment.[2]

Such women, coming off of government aid and hoping to support themselves—after receiving job training, help from mentors, child-care funds, back-to-work wardrobes, make-overs, and lots of enthusiastic support from community organizations and companies—find themselves facing the oppressive tactics of mates who belittle and abuse them. Why? Because holding down a job after depending on government aid is an independent action—a definite sign of separateness, a real Spellbreaker.

People so coerced sometimes give up, succumbing to their mates' control tactics. Or, they may escape but suffer great losses: the loss of children, home, neighborhood, and, at worst, their lives. They don't know why it is that no matter how devoted they are, their mates are so angry at them.

They don't know about "Teddy."

Silencing the Signs of Separateness

When people like the husband in "The Corn Story" attempt to keep Pretend Person anchored in the Witness, they automatically deny the real person's existence.

A Controller's reaction to a sign of separateness could be anywhere on a continuum from verbal abuse to physical violence, both of which create emotional pain and mental anguish.

If the Witness looks in a direction the Controller had not anticipated, or expresses a thought or desire that did not come from the dream person—in other words, that does not reflect the Controller's thinking—the Controller's reaction may range from refusing to speak (as if the Witness is nonexistent) to a raging attack, even violence. All are designed to silence signs of separateness.

It is not always *what* the Witness says or does that triggers such a reaction, but that the Witness says or does anything at all. Since Controllers experience signs of separateness as an outright attack, they will do everything possible to silence the other. This explains a strange paradox. Some people experience engaging comments or questions, such as, "When will you be back?" as incomprehensible attacks, because the question tells them that they and the questioners are not of one mind. Teddy wouldn't have to ask. Teddy would know. Or, would accept not knowing.

One of the most common ways a Controller silences a sign of separateness is to define the *entire authentic self* of the Witness by diminishing or annihilating it in words or actions.

After Betty found that she could not replace her authentic daughter with the "daughter-who-likes-chocolate-walnut-best," she defined her daughter's whole authentic self as "strange."

Your authentic self, to the Pretender, is a "strange" one.

Many Witnesses think that Controllers are rational, so it is not surprising that they believe they can be understood when they explain themselves. But explaining or trying to talk about it with a person who has just defined you ensures increased opposition and invalidation from a confirmed Controller. If spontaneous expressions are threatening, how much more so would be an expression of unhappiness about their controlling behavior?

Witnesses have repeatedly shown themselves to be deeply thoughtful, highly conscious, and careful to express their truth—careful to be authentic. In this way, they are a constant aggravation to the Controller, a constant threat to the Control Connection.

I have heard many people who were caught in Control Connections say that even when they use all their strength to maintain patience, to carefully articulate their truth, to share their deepest feelings, to explain their personal reality to their mates, they don't receive understanding but instead encounter disparagement, subtle trivializing, or outright rage. People with excellent communication skills, sensitivity, and honesty can't "get through."

This is so because when you are sharing your deepest feelings with someone you are *most* authentic. Is anything more authentic than the Witness's pain? Is anything more dislodging of Pretend Person than this kind of authenticity? One would think that such authenticity would break the spell but it rarely does, because the Controller experiences this depth of authenticity as an enormous assault. Consequently, the Controller resists and minimizes it even more than most signs of separateness. Rarely is the Witness's authentic, heartfelt expression accepted as real by the Controller.

I first noticed authenticity as a threat to Controllers when I was struck by the extraordinary authenticity of the vast majority of people who were abused verbally and sometimes physically by their mates.

The "threat" of authenticity often shows up in relationship

counseling. The counselor invites the couple to express their pain to each other. The Controller hears something like "I felt really bad when I heard . . ." and feeling threatened by the appearance of authenticity, the Controller says with real candor, "You're attacking me." Or, conversely, doesn't respond until the session is over, and then, when no one is around, says something like, "You blindsided me!"

If the comment is directed toward someone who isn't familiar with football terms, it is puzzling indeed. A number of people have told me about being so accused. They wondered what it meant. So for the record, it means a "sneak attack." Of course, responding to direction from a counselor in front of the counselor is not sneaky. Being accused in secret is actually more like a "sneak attack," strangely like being "blindsided."

Sudden Separateness

To many Controllers life is a contest, one in which they cannot be defeated. If they see defeat looming, be it in a battle to prove that another's view is wrong, or in a boxing match to prove "superiority," their pretend worlds are about to fall apart. When this happens their illusory connection snaps. Quite often they respond in a violent way to this sudden separateness. "I snapped," they say, to explain their verbally or physically violent reaction—a reaction designed to silence a sign of separateness.

The words "I snapped" clearly describe a response to the experience of sudden separateness and are often used by Controllers to justify desperate attempts to re-establish their illusions, to make their pretend world be their world once again. Now we can all know what "I snapped" means. It means "I am suddenly separate."

Even though Controllers may silence a sign of separateness and momentarily assuage their fear, the fear can always return.

Silencing the authentic person does not end the fear of separateness, because this fear is inside, not outside of those who harbor it.

Since a sign of separateness can appear at any time, Controllers often become vigilant, tense, even depressed. Of course, Witnesses, too, can become depressed, wary, and tense. People in personal contact with Controllers on a regular basis, such as within a family or in the workplace, suffer extraordinarily because it is their very being that threatens the Controller. Hence, they may be assaulted at any time.

Spellbreakers are usually shocked and perplexed if asked what they did to provoke the other when they've been assaulted. If you are ever asked this question, and hopefully you will not be, I suggest you say, "I showed a sign of separateness."

After talking to hundreds of Spellbreakers, I saw that their greatest gifts—eloquence, artistic talent, intellectual genius, common sense—were the very gifts most disparaged by the Controller. Why was this consistently so? Was it some uncanny cruelty? Many Witnesses themselves either didn't truly recognize their gifts or had begun to lose sight of them. Some had even begun to perceive them as their greatest failings. A talented artist I talked with thought he couldn't paint anything worthwhile, his work had been so wholly disparaged. A remarkably eloquent speaker, also disparaged, had become convinced that she "couldn't put two words together." How had the Controllers honed in on the Witnesses' gifts so expertly? To find the answer, I looked through the lens presented in this book. The answer was clear. Controllers expertly target and diminish their Witnesses' greatest gifts because those gifts, like their deepest feelings, are *unusually expressive of their authenticity.* Mozart's musical genius was quite authentically "Mozartish" and certainly demonstrated his separateness.

A popular notion about Controllers is that they give

orders in lieu of requests to protect themselves from the possibility of being turned down. Some literature also attributes such dictatorial behavior to the Controller's fear that if he or she asks for what they want, their request will be subject to negotiation and consequently the Controller won't get his or her way. Another explanation is that asking suggests equality between the Controller and the other. Although all these are of consequence in determining why, for instance, one adult in a couple relationship would presume to give orders to the other, these factors don't fully explain oppressive behavior. An even deeper and more universal causal factor is at work.

Asking gives tacit acknowledgment of the other's separateness. Asking recognizes separateness, breaks the connection. If the Controller asks, he or she faces the threat of severing the Control Connection, of displacing Pretend Person and resurrecting the authentic person—as if the other really were a separate person of whom one could ask something. A dream person like Teddy would always follow orders.

Since asking recognizes the other's autonomy, to some Controllers it is like psychological suicide, and something to be avoided if at all possible. One way to avoid asking is to give orders and to assure compliance by instilling fear in the other. This may be accomplished by acting ferocious, loud, and angry, or by convincing the other that God is behind their imperious behavior. Or the Controller may attempt to gain compliance in a more covert way by withdrawing—threatening the other with emotional abandonment.

This explains why some people who are operating primarily on one function (thinking) promote the idea that they should be in charge of some "four-function" (thinking, feeling, sensate, and intuitive) people—people to whom they want to be connected.

Witnesses who cope with Controllers over years may begin

to ignore their own feelings and intuitions just to avoid the pain of being with someone who tries to control them. Generally, when they fully recognize what has happened and are out of the toxic relationship, they can "get themselves back" as they often decribe their recovery.

Just as *asking* is very difficult for Controllers, so too is *responding*. Controllers withhold responses in order to preserve their Control Connection. Their unconscious "logic" could be, *If I don't respond, I can pretend that you don't exist. I can keep Pretend Person alive and well, anchored in you.* Clearly, responding to Witnesses as if they were separate people severs a Controller's backwards connection and invites a sign of separateness.

Some Controllers, instead of ignoring a question, hear it, but with real frustration.

> *A man said, "Let's have Chinese food."*
> *His wife said, "Okay," but then asked, "Do you want to go out or bring it in?"*
> *Possibly feeling trapped, he shouted angrily, "Why do you have to make it so difficult?"*

If Controllers actually hear a Witness of their own accord, let go of their picture of how a Witness is, and hear the words a Witness speaks just as if she or he truly were a separate person, they usually feel as if they are committing suicide. This is because they have severed their own Control Connection. They have no place to anchor Teddy, and they feel a sudden separateness—separateness from reality itself.

Confusing themselves as much as anyone, some Controllers have adopted a very covert and self-serving strategy by which they solve the problem of response and thereby avoid the terror of disconnection. They only *seem* to respond. Here is how it works.

The Controller says "yes" to a request without accepting it as real. For example, the question, "Will you call if you're going to be late?" is answered with a "yes," but the Controller doesn't follow through and keep the agreement. It is as if the Controller preserves Pretend Person by the following unconscious reasoning.

If I say "yes" to your request, I can leave quickly and won't have to confront your authentic self like I would if I said "no."

I can stay in my dream state with Pretend Person and thus can silence any sign of your separateness.

If I say "no" to your request I'll have to face your authentic self. (And where will Teddy be? Displaced by you!) So I'll say "yes," but of course, I don't have to do what I agreed to. In fact, I won't do it because if I did act on your request I would be acting as if you were real! And where would Teddy be? Gone. I'd be disconnected by me!

I explained this to a man who identified himself as very controlling. He said that now at last he understood why he found it almost impossible to follow through when he had agreed to run an errand for his wife on his way home from work. He said that he always intended to remember. He even put notes on the dashboard of his car, but despite his good intentions he would forget.

Knowing about Pretend Person explains the strange paradox of how some people who present themselves as very helpful and willing seldom, if ever, follow through with their agreements. These are people who frequently say, "Yeah, yeah, yeah, I'll do it." Then they don't do it. In fact, they can be counted on not to do what they said they'd do. It's not that they occasionally forget. It is that they consistently fail to do it. When Witnesses repeat their requests, they often face accusation and denial. They're often told that they're nagging or, conversely, that they never made the request in the first place.

Anytime the Witness seems to be authentic, separate, and real, the Controller experiences a threat to the Control Connection and reacts to the threat by doing everything possible to silence all signs of separateness.

Controllers not only fear separateness but also fear being "found out," that is, discovering that others do not see them as they have made themselves up to be.

Chapter XVIII

The Controller's Indentity Dilemma

If I am right, they must be wrong. I have to be right to exist. I can't have "made myself up" wrong.

Just as signs of separateness threaten the Control Connection, so, too, do they threaten the Controller's identity. Any reality, belief system, or way of being, if it doesn't conform to his or her view, can challenge the Controller.

To allow room for views other than their own would be to open up to an experience that could disrupt, even dismantle, the deep-rooted belief systems on which Controllers base their identity. Their beliefs hold them together, so to speak. Alienated from their inner experience, bereft of self-knowledge and self-acceptance, Controllers increasingly need assurance that they are who they believe themselves to be.

They need this acceptance and agreement from outside themselves because they have made themselves up from the outside in. They oppose Witnesses not only to preserve their Control Connection, but also to preserve their identity.

The Controller's opposition to others' views often takes the form of countering. Countering is verbal opposition that negates the other's opinions, feelings, and beliefs: "You're wrong." "That's not what you're feeling." "That's not what you meant." (See my earlier book, *The Verbally Abusive Relationship: How to Recognize It and How to Respond*, 1996, Adams Media Corporation, for an in-depth look at countering.) Countering prevents relationships, and even though many Controllers know this and really want to stop this oppressive behavior, they often find it extremely difficult to do so. Why? Because different ideas, beliefs, and perceptions—the very appearance of a different "outside"—are threatening to them.

The "outside" is so important to Controllers that they may give up their integrity to gain acceptance, even resort to deception to maintain their image. It is almost a "life or death" issue for them because, just as they mistake the other for a Pretend Person, they mistake themselves for their own image.

The need to be right and the need to look good are closely

related. The following self-revelation is shared by a former Controller turned Spellbreaker. I find its honesty spellbreaking.

> *I would never do anything that might be perceived improper by the general public. In public I wouldn't burst into a rage or demean someone because that would ruin my squeaky-clean image. In public my need to be right was satisfied even when I didn't win if I was seen as a good sport. It's like you can be right but look like an idiot if you lose your cool expressing it. What matters is who sees. And I was a master. No one saw. I deeply needed others to respect me. One of my greatest fears was that someone besides my wife would find out I was behaving improperly.*

Driven by the fear of neither looking good nor of being socially "acceptable," some Controllers spend their lives in pursuit of the "right" clothes, the "right" car, the "right" spouse, and the "right" career. Each of these items, in order to be "right," must fit within a particular scheme of things, fabricated into an identity that substitutes for the one denied them. Conversely, some Controllers reject social mores entirely. In either case Controllers are often at the extreme.

Paradoxically, Controllers usually see themselves as self-reliant even while they are dependent upon others to maintain their backwards connections and their fragile identity. They often carry the banner of rugged independence, of needing no one, while launching an ever-accelerating assault upon someone else's individuality. They are most threatened by Witnesses who do not conform to their particular idea of how things should be.

The outlaw portrayed in movie Westerns could be such a person. He had a gang to affirm his identity. He presented himself as fearless, but depended on his gun for one-upmanship and proof of rightness. He was romanticized but was incapable of having a relationship. He was often presented as a sympathetic character, even a victimized one. And, of course, he wouldn't have done his evil deeds if someone hadn't made him.

His need to maintain his outlaw lifestyle, and to be accepted by and connected to his gang, was so great that it was not unusual for such an outlaw to kill a gang member for leaving him. Leaving in this case is disconnecting, that is, breaking a Control Connection. Killing in this case is a variation on many domestic homicides.

Cultural Prescriptions and Identity Construction

The Spellbound live not only under the influence of the spell, caught in its many illusions, but also under the influence of socially constructed prescriptions that foster and perpetuate Spellbound behaviors. Cultural prescriptions are like formulas that say, "This is how to be." For instance, "You need to wear these clothes to be accepted." "You need to look like this to be beautiful/handsome." "You need to be a _____ to be successful." "You are nobody until somebody loves you."

Such prescriptions influence millions, particularly those who have been left with no recourse other than to make themselves up from the outside in.

Some cultural prescriptions that tell how to manipulate others are: "Don't admit to being wrong." "If you have to admit to being wrong, look good and act nonchalant about admitting it in front of your peers." "Be ready to one-up the person you're with." "Don't admit to not knowing something."

As we move forward let's examine a list of gender prescriptions that tell men specifically how to control women.

Gender Prescriptions

The following correspondence shows a list compiled by two men who were able to recall what they had heard and seen that then became part of their own training to grow up to be men. Knowing that this training contributes to the demise of relationships, and runs counter to all their intentions, they were able to fend off its influence. In the spirit of breaking invisibility on this training, they generously agreed to share their list with me and hence with you. I am confident that when you see it for what it is, you, too, will be able to fend off the influence of this training and/or lessen its impact if it is used against you.

Dear Richard,

I've comprised a list of ways men have been taught to dominate women, as a way to understand the ways in which boys are trained to be men. What do you think?

- Use physical or sexual violence or the threat of physical or sexual violence to get my way.
- Use anger to imply that violence of some form may follow if they don't shut up and do as I want.
- Ignore their experience of male violence from others, adding to their fear of my anger.
- Tell them they're just imagining things when they say they fear my anger—"I've never actually hit you, have I? What on earth are you worried about?"—while conveniently forgetting

that I've demonstrated violence and prevented their escape.

- Use public humiliation and scorn to shame them when with friends and then insist, "I was only joking. Can't you take a joke?"
- Talk hatefully about women in dehumanizing ways with other men. Insist that it isn't really hateful or dehumanizing.
- Use relentless logic to encourage them to deny their own feelings as valid.
- Use relentless logic to deny their feelings of angry frustration when they notice me denying their feelings as valid. (Continue until satisfied with the result.)
- Use their training in body surveillance [wanting to look nice] to gain power over them. For example:
  - Never compliment them. Then say that they mean more to me than just their body.
  - Criticize particular parts of their anatomy whilst insisting that I love them despite these faults (magnanimous until the end).
  - Look at other women with sexually explicit and pornographic gaze.
  - Insist that such a gaze is harmless and doesn't mean anything. "Women watch men's butts, don't they? Aren't we all the same?"
  - Whilst saying that, secretly seduce other women.
- Use women's training in motherhood and looking after men to my material or emotional advantage:

- Insist that it makes them happy to cook, clean, and look after me (despite the awesome weight of evidence that I HATE such tasks).
- If confronted, deny that there is any meaningful difference in shared tasks (after all, I change the fuses).
- Use men's privileged voice to interrupt their sentences constantly, override their ideas, insist that I DO understand these things, have really listened.
- Deny that there is any privilege in my voice. And what are they talking about? "I'm sensitive to women's issues, aren't I? Surely you've seen that? We're no different."
- Provide evidence of being a sensitive guy, become aware of their needs by careful listening, and then:
  - Use this knowledge to seduce them.
  - Use this knowledge to increase my sense of control over them.
  - Use this knowledge to prove that I am no male oppressor (whilst continuing with the more subtle forms).
- When any woman confronts me about any of these issues and dares to question them, argue that I'm a sensitive guy until she gives up. If that doesn't work:
  - Pull out an example of abuse/oppression from my own history and use male privileged voice to demonstrate that it's a people thing, not a gender thing.
  - Find other women to agree with me on this.

- If neither of those work:
  - Express great (preferably genuine) distress and hurt, and insist that this whole subject is just too painful to talk about for me and just makes me feel too accused.
  - Demand or trick women to take care of my distress over this topic.
  - Insist that she discuss these issues with me in calm ways, that aren't too accusatory or angry in case it upsets me so much that I can't listen anymore. It's okay for her to be angry when I think I'm strong enough to take it, as long as she allows me to walk away from it if I need to.
- Deny the reality of gender oppression or say it is just being politically correct or is already sorted, so it's no problem.
- Deny that any of these trainings exist.
- Admit to the more obvious tactics but don't admit that the subtle ones exist.
- Pretend that this is a complete list.
- Convince myself that now that I've written this list, I'm immune to it.
- Paralyze myself with guilt and shame now that I've figured out I've done all these things myself.
- Demand or trick her to take care of my distress over this topic.

I suspect that I've just scratched the surface.

Glen Simblett
Hamilton, New Zealand

Dear Glen,

In response to your astonishing catalogue of common practices through which men dominate women, I'd like to add a few more to the list.

I try to keep a running catalogue in my head, but I forget a lot. Your list has helped me retrieve some.

- Devalue the woman by:
  - Not listening to what she has to say, or
  - Listening in a preoccupied or distracted way, without asking questions or showing any interest. Look impatient and put-upon.
- Find fault with what she says, or imply that she should have done it better, known more, etc.
- If she complains that you don't spend enough time talking to her, persuade her that she's too needy and demanding, or
  - Use the opportunity to get her to listen to your worries and stresses as an explanation for why you can't be more available to her. Suggest that she doesn't appreciate how much you do for her in other ways—for example, working hard and contributing financially to the family.
- If you make more money than she makes, claim that this gives you the right to have greater say in how money is spent.
- If she is asking you to take on more responsibility or do more work around the house, ask what she is going to do for you in exchange. In any negotiation, both people have to compromise, right? Deny any overall imbalance in the distribution of labor or responsibility.

- Ask rhetorical, prosecutorial questions.
- If confronted on your criticism, deny that you were being critical (I was only asking an innocent question. . .) and,
  - Imply that she is being overly sensitive or,
  - Make her feel guilty for misperceiving your intentions and hurting your feelings.

I don't wish to convey the idea, by constructing this list, that I see men as consciously or deliberately intending these behaviors to have the effects they customarily have, though some men do use these strategies with conscious purpose and with an intent to dominate. I think most men who engage in these practices think of themselves as nice guys, thoughtful, considerate, well-meaning.

Richard Maisel, Ph.D.
Berkeley, California

From the perspective of this book, the list reveals four primary ways to maintain a Control Connection. (1) Frighten the authentic person with displays of rage and similar behaviors in order to silence signs of separateness. (2) Manipulate the authentic person to act like Pretend Person. (3) Diminish the authentic person in order to make room for a Pretend Person. (4) Confuse the authentic person, in order to turn him or her into a Pretend Person; that is, encourage her to lose her own mind so she will be of one mind with the Controller.

Needless to say, cultural prescriptions formulated by people who are disconnected from themselves and who have built their identities from the outside in, backwards, suggest that backwards approaches and backwards connections are unquestionably appropriate. That they are just the way it is. Not surprisingly, such prescriptions foster a controlling lifestyle.

I asked a woman who had once been caught in a Control Connection with a man who had been under the influence of these cultural prescriptions to describe the effects of these practices. In less than sixty seconds she poured forth the following: "horrifying, mental torture, mental anguish, mind scrambling, painful confusion, bewilderment, torture, worse than active or remembered violence."

Unlike the two men who contributed the list, many people don't comprehend the impact of controlling behaviors. Controllers themselves certainly don't view their behaviors as cruel or particularly hurtful, so absorbed are they in trying to maintain their dominance, their built-backwards identities, and their backwards connections.

All indications are that men seem to face more mandates to maintain Control Connections than do women. But women too may emulate the behaviors on the list.

Also, some women may develop their identities backwards by modeling themselves on the stereotype of "feminine mindlessness and helplessness." These women make themselves up in accordance with a cultural prescription for a female dream person. (A Barbie doll? An all-need-meeting mother/father?) They are easy targets for Controllers. They try to get what they want by being a "dream woman," and in that way try to control their mate's behavior, that is, gain their mate's love. Still, no matter how much they try to fill the role of dream woman, they cannot succeed. No one can be an illusion.

Some of women's erroneous cultural prescriptions around the issue of control in relationships are the following:

- Flatter and act nice to your man, and don't act too smart to make sure he feels important like a man "should," and then he'll be happy and he'll stay with you, because you really can't get along without him.

- Be sure to learn to type just in case you can't keep him and you end up alone—a sign that you just weren't good enough, or weren't helpless enough and didn't follow this prescription well enough.
- Stay thin and make the relationship work because if you love him enough it will work.

Some parents make up dream children, defining them, telling them what they think, feel, want, and so forth. This is emotionally toxic to the child, as it is to any Witness.

At an elegant dinner I heard a seventy-year-old man tell his forty-year-old daughter, who was going sailing the next weekend with a new suitor, "Don't let him know you're a champion. Let him think he's better at sailing."

For the most part, women's erroneous cultural prescriptions help maintain the spell because they reinforce men's erroneous cultural prescriptions.

As a result of these prescriptions, some men are afraid or unable to show warmth, gentleness, flexibility, openness, and vulnerability. They fear not meeting the requirements of being a "man," of being tough enough to be accepted by the generations of men who could not show them their own gentleness—the generations that, in turn, sought acceptance by conforming to other men's requirements. They fear that if they opened the door to their feelings, intuitions, and sensations, they would not only have to accept all they had learned to scorn in themselves, but also lose their identities.

Now we'll look more closely at the Controller's fears.

Chapter XIX

Fear

*Our protections from fear
may be more to be feared
than fear itself.*

When Controllers are beside themselves because they are not "within" themselves, it is almost as if they have no "within." Bereft of primary sources of information, they lose access to their inner worlds and seek self-knowledge from outside of themselves. They fear their own experience, because it comes by way of the functions they have been taught to disregard: their feelings, sensations, and intuitions.

Feelings seem dangerous to Controllers, who have been trained to believe that emotions are wrong, not real, not to be acknowledged, trusted, or even contemplated, and to believe that if they show their pain or even their pleasure, they will be wounded further.

While the Teddy Illusion can protect them from feeling disconnected, Controllers are often severely controlling even of themselves, keeping their emotions at bay by repressing or ignoring them through willful effort and chosen distraction. If by chance their emotions do emerge, rising on a tide so great they cannot be kept back, Controllers will likely think it is someone else's fault. Anger, anxiety, and emotional pain do not, to their minds, have anything to do with their disconnection or unreasonable expectations. Taking no responsibility for their actions, Controllers are prone to say, "You made me do it. It's all your fault."

Sometimes people have so completely closed the door on their feelings that they do not know what feelings feel like. They fear feelings and, in some cases, their fear resembles paranoia. The following is a worst-case scenario, but a real account of fear that has reached a paranoid level. The husband in this account, instead of dealing with his own fears, did everything possible to terrorize his wife. Could it have been that he wanted her to experience as much fear as he felt so that he could see it "out there" instead of within himself?

A gentle woman, who by her own account was very naive, told me her story, in a whispered and hurried way. Remarried several years after the loss of her loving first husband in a tragic accident, she soon realized that her new husband was seemingly taken over by paranoia. He was extremely oppressive. He monitored her every phone call, directed her every move, and manipulated her into her present penniless position.

He seemed to be so afraid she might find an interest outside of her marriage, or have the means to escape from the marriage itself, that he took every possible measure to prevent even the possibility of such an occurrence.

From our perspective, it seems he feared losing the body that harbored his dream woman as much as he would fear losing himself.

When she expressed dissatisfaction, he did not threaten her life, but told her that if she ever left him, he would see that her young daughter was injured to the point of living in a "vegetable" state. He said that every time she'd see her child she'd be reminded that she shouldn't have left. Because he had wealth (her money now, too), prestige in their community, and access to drugs, she knew that he could make good on his threat.

His fear created a new fear in her, and the more she feared her husband, the more secure he seemed to be. But because her fear for herself and her child grew, her desire for their freedom also grew. Beneath the surface of her days, she constantly searched for a way to escape to another part of the world.

In the midst of our conversation, she heard him arrive home and she hung up the phone.

I do not know the outcome of this woman's dilemma, nor even what country she called from. I had heard great fear in her voice and was so moved by this anonymous woman's account that I decided to share it here to illustrate the husband's paranoia, the kind of fear that claims to justify jealous rages and the most tightly clenched Control Connections.

To some Controllers, physical sensations are as suspect as emotions themselves, in part because feelings are often expressed through our bodies. In a sensate way, we experience the sinking feeling of something terribly wrong, the rush of adrenaline when danger threatens, the heart pain of grief.

Physical sensations not only tell us about ourselves from the inside out, but also suggest a vulnerability that doesn't demonstrate power over self or others. And such vulnerability, revealed, does not foster acceptance by other Controllers of similar mindset. If you have adopted a controlling lifestyle, you must prove that you are "tough enough." If you are living with a Controller, you may just not be.

While some Controllers revel in what they see as their sophisticated tastes, others fear revealing even the slightest sensitivity. The pleasure of the delicate and complex are to be ignored. The scent of a flower, the beauty of fine art and classical sounds cannot be appreciated, because such awareness arises from within, the territory of dreaded "inner experience," and possibly the feminine.

At the other end of the spectrum, far from sensitivity, some people also block awareness of even great physical pain. Fearing sensate experience, not feeling their pain until they collapse, they risk their health to "win," to practice shutting down their sensate function.

Some people fear and even scorn one of the most powerful inner experiences: the experience of intuition. Because intuitive knowledge arrives instantly, fully processed from the inside out, it truly points to there being a "within," a "place" Controllers shun. And it is thought by some to be a feminine attribute—not suitable to a man.

Women too can fall under the influence of this cultural prescription, thinking no one should attend to their intuition. Even healthy women, connected to themselves and not subject to the assults of a Controller, can doubt their intuition if it is not highly regarded in their culture. The following is an account of a woman being told by another woman, an authority figure, to disregard her intuitive knowledge.

> *Lea contacted me for support. She told me that her therapist had said, "What are you going to do, trust your* inner knowings *or me? After all, you've paid me to evaluate the situation. I'm your therapist. You should follow my advice."*
>
> *Lea's therapist had seen her twice, but even if it had been twenty times, such an assertion would not have been therapeutic. It could well be dangerous. In this case Lea's mate, Vic, had convinced the therapist he really loved Lea. Lea's therapist didn't know about Teddy. She didn't know whom Vic really loved. Vic didn't either. Vic's efforts to turn Lea into Teddy became violent.*
>
> *Lea wanted to be loved for herself, but since no one could explain Vic to himself, Vic didn't know what to do. He was plugged in and powerless. He felt constantly attacked. Signs of separateness seemed to appear out of nowhere. He tried harder and harder to put them down and so put Lea down. All to be close.*

Please note that many therapists encourage self-trust. But many people have learned to distrust their own intuition and everyone else's, too. It was not so long ago that those who listened to their intuition were called witches and warlocks. They were condemned by a culture that did not know that inner knowing was the essential outcome of natural connection and was also affirmation of that connection. Essential because intuition can save a person's life and an affirmation because intuition, rightly read, speaks the truth of inner-connectedness.

Before we even had a word for intuition, people thought that their own intuitive knowing was a message from some celestial being. Even now, "gods" and "goddesses" are used by some to explain away the voice of intuition. But when accepted, our intuition can speak wisdom in a multitude of languages.

Our well-being requires that we become acquainted with our inner knowings and how to respond to them. They can be life-saving. In Gaven de Becker's book, *The Gift of Fear*, number one on his list of "pre-incident indicators associated with spousal violence and murder" is: *"The woman has intuitive feelings that she is at risk."*[3]

Controllers have other fears besides the fear of inner experience. And, they have particular needs that, if met, temporarily protect them from these fears. Primarily, Controllers fear being wrong and being inferior. Hence they need to be right and to win. We'll look at these needs and how they arise out of fear.

The Need to Be Right

If you did not *know* yourself from within, but had made yourself up mostly from the outside without reference to your experience, you would be threatened by different views. You would be threatened not only because they are signs of separateness, but also because you would need to be assured that you had made yourself up "right." Controllers often tell Spellbreakers, "You always have to be right," with the intention of getting them to give up their own view.

If someone built his identity backwards and found out he was "wrong" about anything, what would happen to his identity? To the Spellbound, being wrong about anything means likewise being wrong about themselves: an identity-shattering experience.

A client said, "If I'm wrong my whole being is wrong."

As the Spellbound fight the fear of being wrong, many Witnesses wonder if *they* are doing something wrong. Some women have been taught in hundreds of ways that they are wrong about what they do. Wrong to speak up. Wrong to object. Wrong to pursue certain careers. Wrong to express an opinion. Wrong to question. Wrong to appear able. These teachings, however, are what is wrong. *They are the spell at work.* These messages can leave a person feeling paralyzed, unable to act, or at least unable to act without permission.

Some men, on the other hand, are taught in hundreds of ways that they are wrong to attend to and acknowledge their inner experiences, but right about whatever they do. These teachings are also wrong. They deepen the spell.

All else being equal, people who have been able to remain connected to themselves and to develop their identities from the inside out don't have a problem finding out that they are wrong about something. They know they are still "there," because they know themselves from their experience. But being wrong does not even seem to be an option to the Spellbound. Their unconscious assumption is, "If you're right then I'd have to be wrong, and I'm not. We can't both be right with different views. If I'm wrong about anything, then who am I? The 'I' that I know is annihilated."

Being right is doubly important to anyone anchored in another via a Pretend Person, because in this circumstance being right annihilates any sign of separateness. Being right affirms the establishment of a one-mind, one-view connection.

A man explained how he tried to get his wife to give up her reality. His sole purpose in sharing this information is to break the spell.

> *Even if I knew I was wrong—and yes, sometimes I did know but denied it—it was important to me to look better than my wife. I needed to win at all costs. I wanted support from my wife. That is exactly why I wanted her to be of one mind with me. I couldn't support her if she wasn't. And that's exactly why being right and winning was so critical. When the prospect of winning was dim, I would lose control in abusive anger that, I think, was more like an all-out assault to win. When I lost control of myself, she would do whatever it took to end the episode, even admitting she was wrong, even if she wasn't. I would walk away secured by her.*

Interestingly, being "secured by her" is quite similar to being "anchored in her."

At any time, of course, Controllers may face their fears and with courage and support they will find out that they don't die when their mates have different views. Going through the experience of "not dying" builds inner-connectedness. When this inner-connecteness begins to develop, *breaking the spell is always an option.*

The Need to Be One Up

Being "one up" depends upon an assumption of hierarchy: that one person is superior to another and therefore, won't be challenged about being right.

People who have made themselves up backwards usually unconsciously assume that other people have also made themselves up. It is then only a small step to pretend that the other is lesser and that they are greater, and to further pretend that saying it's so makes it so, or even to pretend that if they are convincing, *it will be so.*

When Controllers say something like "you're stupid," they may believe not only that they have made it so by saying it's so, but also that if they have put someone down they have put themselves up. This view is common in the pretend world of Controllers. It is often seen in children trying to "connect" with others by bullying, teasing, and taunting. When a Witness gives up trying to convince a Controller that he or she is not "stupid," the Controller believes he or she is one up and has won.

But not for long, I think.

The Need to Win

Have you ever spent time with someone who seemed to need to argue against everything you said, just to win, just to get you to give up your view? Or, even if you had the same opinion as your self-appointed opponent, did he or she still cast you as the adversary? Did this person use "relentless logic," as described earlier, to get you to deny your feelings? If so, you have encountered a Spellbound person exercising his or her need to win. The need to win exists only because the Spellbound, having made themselves up backwards, need to prove they are "right." And of course at the moment that they try to prove themselves, they become oppressive. The Controller's need to be right is even greater than his or her need to be honest.

Although winning at a game can be fun, and gives most of us a feeling of having both skill and good fortune, winning is more than a game to Controllers. Controllers who battle the authenticity of others must also battle their disowned authentic self and bury its one-down feeling with a win.

Controllers need to win to prove themselves strong enough and able enough to withstand Spellbreakers. Anyone to whom they have connected backwards could at any moment sever the connection, show signs of separateness or, by having a different opinion, lifestyle, or idea, challenge the rightness of the Controller's identity.

Chapter XX

Control Tactics

One need not think to employ control tactics.

M ost Controllers don't plan to control anyone. Nevertheless, they do everything they can to keep their Pretend Person alive and well. When Controllers spot a sign of separateness, they are angry and frightened by the appearance of an authentic person, and their response is to try to control the authentic person.

Tightening Their Grip

When Controllers encounter Witnesses' authenticity, particularly in familial relationships, they begin to feel the disconnection they are trying to avoid. Consequently, besides needing to be right, to be one up and to preserve their identities, they need to tighten their grip. Normally when people confront difficult situations, they get a grip on themselves by drawing upon their inner resources. But the Controller gets a grip within another. The Controller usually tries to accomplish this by defining the authentic person: "You're just trying to get attention, wasting time, and causing a scene."

It is as if the Controller is saying, "Since I've made you up, I know what goes on within you and since you don't act the way you 'should,' I'll tell you what is wrong with you so you'll know how you're supposed to be, i.e., my Pretend Person (my Teddy)."

Each time Controllers do this, they feel more secure, and, for a while, even feel happy with the other whom they now see as the Pretend Person they love. *"Everything seems normal."* Thus the abuse may appear to run in cycles. The Controller's increasing experience of disconnection has been assuaged for the moment but may return in a little while.

If their first attempt to tighten their grip is resisted, Controllers try even harder, being even more annihilating of the authentic person.

Do you recall how the husband in "The Corn Story" defined his wife's ability to count change? When his authentic wife said "Guess it's too early . . ." she had suddenly displaced Pretend Wife (Teddy). Teddy would never be less than perfect! Consequently the husband's anchor and Control Connection were at risk. He felt dislodged. He felt *attacked*. He wanted to get close, to have Teddy back. Recall his anger at his authentic wife: "She can't even count the goddamn change." He diminished her, both to explain his anger and to *make room* for his pretend wife (Teddy). And even though his authentic wife said nothing (seeming almost to disappear), when he learned his definition was being questioned by others, he met his need to *tighten his grip* by defining his wife again, this time *all-inclusively*: "My wife, the war zone."

Although Witnesses are not war zones, their psyches have become the locale of many a battle between themselves and Pretend Persons. People who return to a controlling relationship nearly always experience even more oppressive behavior, because the Controller re-anchors Teddy, tightening his or her grip within the Witness, making sure that Teddy won't get away again!

Diminishing

To feel securely anchored, the Controller must *make room* for Pretend Person in the Witness's body by attempting to diminish, make smaller, the authentic person who resides there. "You're nothing" or "you're a zero" are the kinds of comments that reflect the Controller's desire to erase the Witness. The Controller is compelled to make sure, at least in his or her pretend world, that there is room for Teddy and that no one else lives within the psychic boundary of the Witness.

Even though many Witnesses cling to their own reality and know that they are not really diminished, this kind of abuse in a relationship eventually takes a psychic and physical toll on the recipient.

Isolating

Controllers respond to resistance instantaneously, and they try to protect themselves from those occasions where they may meet with resistance. In one-to-one Control Connections, if Controllers can isolate the Witness, it is easier for them to avoid resistance and to tighten their grip. With no Spellbreakers around, they can maintain their illusion. The following is an example:

> Arri asked, "Just when I became successful in the preschool I opened, he wanted me to quit and seemed angry about my success. My children were grown and I was home by mid-afternoon. Why wasn't he happy for me?"
>
> "Did you meet many people in this work?" I asked.
>
> "Yes, actually I was pretty well known in the community."
>
> "Then might he have seen other people seeing you as if you were a real person?" I asked.
>
> "Oh, I see." she said. "There were as many signs of my separateness as there were people who saw me."

Controllers find themselves further and further adrift, more deeply threatened, even as they strive to affirm their rightness, their one-up position and their victories. With no knowledge of the spell, what can they do but tighten their grip and blame others for their behavior?

Verbal Abuse: A Control Tactic

Let's see how verbal abuse specifically relates to the preservation of Pretend Person. Teddy, in these examples, is a Pretend Person of any age or gender.

- If the Controller uses an anger tactic in combination with any of the tactics mentioned in this chapter, the Controller is feeling threatened and wants Teddy back.
- If the Controller uses a withholding tactic, it is as if the Controller is saying, "You are not to be acknowledged or responded to. You don't exist. I want to stay in my dream state with Teddy."
- If the Controller uses a name-calling tactic, it is as if the Controller is saying, "You are specifically something other than who you are. You're not a person. Only Teddy is real."
- If the Controller uses a blaming or accusing tactic, it is as if the Controller is saying, "If only you'd be Teddy and quit attacking me by appearing as an authentic person, I wouldn't have to say or do this. I have a good 'reason' to behave as I do."
- If the Controller uses a judging, criticizing, or disparaging tactic, it is as if the Controller is saying, "You are not who you perceive yourself to be. I define you because you are not a self-defining person. You should be Teddy."
- If the Controller uses a trivializing tactic, it is as if the Controller is saying, "You, your opinion, your work, or your interests are nothing but signs of separateness. I want my Teddy whose interests are the same as mine."
- If the Controller uses a threatening, undermining, ordering, countering, blocking, or diverting tactic, it is as if the Controller is saying, "You may not be yourself.

You may not have, or pursue, your query, your course of action, or your thought. You may not exist as a separate person. Only my Teddy knows how to think and act."

It is important to know that being speechless from trauma is not the same as withholding. Withholding is a purposeful refusal to respond appropriately and is designed to punish the Witness by threatening withdrawal from the relationship.

Similarly, being angry at a Controller and even shouting "stop it" to control tactics is not the same as abusive anger designed to control the other through fear and intimidation.

Stalking

We hear of people stalking their former or imagined lovers or spouses, or stalking celebrities or people who simply seem accessible to the stalker. Statistics reveal that a woman is most at risk when she leaves an abusive mate, because he may stalk and attack her.[4]

Some people have speculated that stalking has something to do with a primal male hunting instinct because so many women are stalked. But since women have been stalkers, too, we see stalking as the Control Connection at a distance.

It is first and foremost an attempt to keep a grip on a Pretend Person via a real person. Controllers stalk their target because they don't want to lose a place to anchor Teddy. Once a Pretend Person is anchored in an authentic person, the stalker doesn't want it to get away. *Where did Teddy go?*

Stalkers can be relentless and obsessive. Even when stalkers pursue a stranger, the stalker "knows" how the other "should" be, how they feel and so forth. They "know" because the target (authentic person) has become a "Pretend Person" in the stalker's mind.

Commonly, when stalkers see their target respond by looking over a shoulder, changing their phone number, or speeding away, the stalker feels connected. The stalking behavior has brought about a direct response. The stalker is now "in the mind" of the target, just where the stalker wanted to be all along. *We're so close.*

Some stalkers kill the person they're stalking. It is as if the stalker is unconsciously thinking, "You won't be the way I want you to be. My Pretend Person is gone. You're ruining everything." Or, "You're making me do this. I'll get you if it's the last thing I do." Hence a stalker may kill to keep Teddy from getting away. Tragically, when death is the final outcome of a Control Connection, a crime scene is the final proof of a backwards connection.

I've heard many stories from women being stalked. One woman recently told me that she was being stalked for the fourth time. She trembled and cried. She had never even met her current stalker. She was only twenty-one.

Another woman, divorced from her stalker, received this chilling message: "It won't be over 'till you're with me, and if it's the grave, that's how it'll be."

Road Rage

Action against strangers is another form of the Control Connection at a distance. Most people are familiar with one of its common manifestations, road rage. Controllers take action against those who don't conform to their picture of how they should be. In the 1990s, the media alerted U.S. citizens to a rash of road rage incidents, which can be defined as an act of violence by a driver against another driver precipitated by remarkably trivial incidents.

An American Automobile Association study of road rage

found that the assailants were agitated by small, spontaneous, or neutral acts such as: the victim's driving slower or closer than the assailant imagined to be appropriate; the victim's turning where the assailant imagined he or she shouldn't have turned, the victim's parking where the assailant imagined he or she shouldn't have parked, and so forth.[5]

Through the lens of this book, we notice that the victims showed signs of separateness. They failed to be Pretend People. They failed to do what the assailants imagined they should do.

The assailants created a pretend world populated by Pretend People who drove the way they were "supposed" to drive. When these perfect Pretend People disappeared, when the assailants were resisted by reality—the separate acts of separate people—they were enraged, not unlike a man we'll soon meet who was enraged by the small, spontaneous, neutral, and separate act of his wife: "I'd like the linguini."

Chapter XXI

Confabulation

*One of the most difficult
obstacles to coping with
a person built backwards is
the person's unawareness that
they've connected backwards.*

To an astonishing extent, Controllers seem to believe themselves when they excuse their oppressive behaviors: "It was what they did, the way they looked, the way they said it, or what they really meant, that made me do it!" Or "I didn't do anything!"

Every week someone tells me something like Mr. D's account:

> *I convinced a psychiatrist and two therapists, Ph.D.s, that I was fine and my wife was nutty.*
>
> *All my friends and coworkers admire me as a terrific guy. But I've faced my first arrest and owned up to my friends. I've got a major problem that's been going on for quite a while. They can hardly believe it.*

As Controllers tighten their grip within the other, the spell has a firmer grip on them. When Mr. D. had time to consider his behavior, he realized that he didn't know why he did what he did, why he had ignored, challenged, and attempted to diminish, define, and annihilate his authentic wife. Here is another example:

> *A man I'll call Joe came to my office for help. I soon saw that, as candid as he was about his behavior, he too could not really understand himself.*
>
> *He had gone out to dinner the previous evening with his wife and some friends. His wife ordered an entrée she really loved. "I'd like the linguini," she said.*
>
> *Hearing her, Joe told me, he was overcome with anger. He "blew up." But his behavior seemed justified to him at the time because it hadn't occurred to him that his wife wouldn't know what he wanted her to order.*
>
> *I asked him how she responded.*

"She became really quiet. She excused herself and then came back in about ten minutes. Then she talked to everyone but me. Later when we were driving home, she said she'd felt real bad. I told her to quit complaining."

I talked with Joe about his wife's pain. Then I asked, "Now that you know that she felt hurt, shocked, and totally disregarded, do you feel inclined to apologize and talk to her about it?"

"I can't really do that."

Why is that?

"Because then she'll know it really happened."

Joe was a neighborly, friendly kind of guy. Not crazy. Joe had just become so used to his dream wife, so used to telling his real wife "how it is," so securely anchored in her, he seemed to have forgotten that his authentic wife existed at all. Most significant, he still thought that if he didn't tell her what happened, she wouldn't know!

Joe's rage was actually his reaction to a sign of separateness: his wife's spontaneous remark. "I'll have the linguini." (Teddy doesn't make spontaneous remarks all on her own.)

As I explained the Control Connection to him, he began to see that his behavior wasn't justified. Now as he sat across from me, he said that he could see that she was just being a person placing an order at a restaurant. At the time though, he had felt that she had attacked him. After all, Teddy wouldn't have come up with an order like that, not when he was thinking of splitting pizza. Teddy would have *known* what he wanted.

Joe worked diligently to monitor his behavior, listening with respect, following the course of study I recommended. Gradually he overcame the spell's influence.

Knowing that he or she has acted irrationally doesn't

immediately enable the Controller to stop oppressive behaviors. It takes time.

Zee, in a state of confusion, revealed his intelligence and willingness to overcome the influence of the spell. As we talked he shared much of himself.

> "I didn't treat anyone like I treated her," he said. "Everyone I've told, my family and friends, are incredulous. They've never seen this side of me! I don't understand it myself. For instance, even after I knew how I treated her, and we were giving it one more try, I was still cruel to her. Why?" he asked, plaintively.
>
> "I'd like to know just what happened. Can you tell me about it?" I asked.
>
> "She promised to stay and see if we could work things out over the next month. Around then, she asked how my day had gone and said she'd love to hear a little of what I do.
>
> "I knew I'd closed her out of my life [Zee had a fascinating career], so I told her I'd be back in a little while and we could talk. Ten minutes later I came in and, seeing her, said in the most sarcastic way I could, 'So, now, I'll tell you aaalll about my trip to the hardware store.'
>
> "She said, 'You just don't get it. You just don't get it.' And left."
>
> "What compels me to act like that? I humiliated and hurt her and I don't know why. I'm a real Dr. Jekyll/Mr. Hyde personality."

I told him about Pretend Person, the Teddy Illusion, and the fear of facing the "authentic person" and losing the Control Connection.

Zee's wife, deeply traumatized from many similar incidents, had left for good, but Zee, realizing full well why, said, "All I can do is support her in her plans. I can't blame her. It'll take me time to change."

Zee did help his wife leave and set about getting well.

Unlike Zee, other Controllers, not knowing that they have established a Control Connection, not knowing that they fear the other's separateness, not even knowing why they do what they do—may confabulate "reasons" for their assaults and even for all that has transpired.

Confabulation

We now confront a strange paradox: A person can believe that they are enraged by something they've actually just "made up." Recall how the husband in the "Corn Story" was enraged when his wife was uncertain about the amount of money she received in change. He said that his wife "couldn't count the goddamn change." He confabulated this as a "reason" for his anger. The real reason for his rage was that his wife had said something spontaneously, something that didn't come from him, something he didn't expect, and something Teddy wouldn't say.

Not knowing why he was angry, his mind gave him a "reason." This is confabulation.

Similarly, in "The Teddy Illusion," the Controller felt rage when Teddy said "When will you be back?" and blamed Teddy for his feeling, confabulating, "All you do is question me."

When people are beside themselves, they are not likely to know and remember what happened when they weren't "there." It is as if they have a lapse of memory. When this happens, their mind can automatically confabulate what transpired or can confabulate a "reason" for what they are feeling.

To see how this happens, I invite you to imagine suddenly finding yourself in a store but unable to remember how you got there. Almost before you know that you don't know, your mind can confabulate a "reasonable" explanation. "I took the bus and dozed on the way." This happens so you don't feel crazy or panicked over losing your memory.

If you are overcome with an extremely powerful rage as if you've been attacked, but no actual attack has occurred, your mind may confabulate a "reason" for your feeling.

The psychiatric diagnostic manual describes a diagnosis that fits quite well: "Amnesiac disorder not otherwise specified. It is evidenced by the recital of imaginary events to fill in gaps in memory."

Confabulations allow us to feel sane when we wouldn't otherwise. *Confabulations seem like actual memory,* seem to be the truth to the person who confabulates. Confabulations are so like actual memory that when a person confabulates a reason for, say, anger, he or she thinks that it actually is the reason for the anger. No wonder physical and verbal abusers so often appear to be telling the truth when they explain away their hurtful behavior.

Confabulation has an eerie and mind-boggling effect on Witnesses. When people hear untruth spoken as truth, it is as if they had stepped into an unreal world.

No one wants to be displaced by a Pretend Person or to suffer the effects of the Controller's identity dilemma. No one wants to come under the influence of anyone or any group that is under the influence of the spell. But unsuspecting people have. Great numbers of people have lost their lives physically or spiritually because they fell under the influence of people who were Spellbound, and some people who might have spoken out did not, and some who did were silenced. Whole cultures did not see the spell descending.

In the miller's story the question is, "How sick was the culture that gave a man the right to act in a way that affected his family without first consulting them?"

The miller's power over others was culturally mandated, approved by the Spellbound to preserve the spell. Whenever a culture is so sick that it normalizes this level of disregard, it is already deeply under the spell.

Sometimes it is only when the Controller has fought to the death to displace authentic person and establish Pretend Person that others discover control was involved. When people do make this discovery, they may still wonder, "What provoked this?"

Whether or not we have come to understand Control Connections, we naturally resist the person who "makes us up." We resist the person who pretends to have said what wasn't said, or pretends not to have said what was said. We resist the person who leaves us feeling uneasy. We resist even when we're not quite sure why it is that we feel resistant.

If we are aware, we respond appropriately, speak up, leave quietly, run, even plan escapes, whether from oppressive regimes or oppressive relationships.

Consequently, the Spellbound face resistance all of their lives. As they fight to survive they sink further under the weight of the spell. Having no solid ground on which to stand, no inner connection, they live with the constant threat of disconnection. The outcome is their increasing need to be right, to be one up, to win, and to tighten their grip.

They wage a constant battle and bear an increasing burden. In a very real sense, the Spellbound move against life itself. It is not easy to affirm Pretend Person or other persons or events while simultaneously remaining unconscious of the fact that one is immersed in an illusion. Some Controllers persist without regard to means or consequence. This, in some cases, is a fight unto death, often explained by a confabulation.

Once a "reason" is confabulated, the Controller may go one step further. The Controller may seek agreement from others. How else to stay sane in a world of resistance? How else to manage living under the spell?

When a person seeks agreement with another person to align with them against someone or some group, his or her Control Connection is magnified. We'll enter this new territory in the next part of our journey.

Part III

This is a new juncture in our journey of exploration through the maze of senseless behaviors woven into our world. We are leaving one-to-one Control Connections to enter the territory of group connections—the controlling kind that create mass havoc throughout the world. We'll find out what happens when Spellbound people get together, and the far-reaching impact of these "close" connections.

Even though we'll be in a different climate with different foliage, all Control Connections essentially take root in the same soil. We'll explore them down to their source so as not to be caught off-guard should we encounter two or more Spellbound people at the same time. Later, after we've seen these connections up close we'll discover the compelling force behind them and all Control Connections.

Chapter XXII

Other "Close" Connections

Pretending together
seems even better
than pretending alone.

G lancing back for a moment, we have seen that people who indulge in oppressive behaviors approach others and even connect to others in a backwards way. And, since these people have become disconnected from themselves, they've even constructed their identity backwards, from the outside in.

Because they are Spellbound, they don't know how senseless their behaviors are. And, paradoxically, because they are Spellbound, they are driven to keep themselves Spellbound. Their struggle is constant and they don't know why.

They must maintain their illusory connection *and* their built-backwards identity. Tragically, because of their illusions, they find many of life's ordinary experiences threatening. We will now take a look at group contol connections. As we move into this new group territory, we'll take a look at healthy groups, for the sake of contrast.

Healthy Groups

Healthy groups are bonded together *for*, not against, others. Most of us enjoy being part of a group. We feel a sense of connection when we have joined with others toward a particular purpose. A healthy group is supportive of each member, is not harmful to others, and functions within the context of an agreed-upon meaning and purpose. It is not isolated, may be large or small, and may have begun with two people bonded together for some purpose.

Members are open to the exchange of information among themselves and with other groups. Groups are part of human society. Humanity is, of course, a group composed of groups. In order for a group to function, members are expected to keep their agreements, even if it is only showing up on time or staying informed of current events and making choices at the polls.

There are many kinds of groups, including interest groups,

rights groups, and work-related groups. Families are also groups. Members are bonded at a deeper level than are interest groups or work-related groups. Members of a family rely upon each other to share responsibilities and to emotionally support each other in a context of respect and goodwill.

In a broad sense, the citizens of cities and countries also make up groups. Collectively, they may form alliances or bonds with other groups, establishing new connections. They are bonded in a much less tangible way than the members of a family.

Unhealthy Groups

In contrast to healthy groups, unhealthy groups are bonded together *against,* rather than for, another person or group. Such bonding can begin with just two people. It is not difficult to imagine how much a person who is disconnected would want to feel doubly connected—for instance, connected to a Pretend Person or persons and also connected to someone else or some group who shared his or her illusion, or even connected to a person or group that *might* share his or her illusion.

People can bond together against others in very informal and subtle ways as well as in very organized ways. We'll look at some informal ways of bonding against others before we move on to explore more formally organized ones.

When two or more people *define* another person or group, they actually bond together against that person or group. This bond, like any Control Connection, is a sick substitute for real connection. It is based upon an illusion. It says, so to speak, "We will pretend that we know who or what that person is, or should be, or that we know what is best for them."

The following is an example that may already have occurred to you. If after the man in "The Corn Story" said "My wife, the war zone," I had said, "Yeah, she sure is," I would have shared his illusion, and we would have formed a *bond together against* his authentic wife. Having dispensed with his partner, the husband would have felt more closely bonded to his illusory Pretend Person. And also, most significant, he would have felt bonded with me *against* her. *A doubly sick connection.*

Bonding together against others is, like all Control Connections, a backwards connection. The bond is based upon an agreement, sometimes unspoken, to act or to be against an authentic person or persons in order to sustain an illusion. For example, when a bully says something diminishing and defining of someone passing by and another person joins in laughing at the crude remark, the bully has gained agreement. Of course, what was said was nonsensical and illusory. Bonding together against others often begins when two people fall under the spell in this way. In effect, they share the same illusion.

People who practice bigotry depend upon certain groups to give them meaning, purpose, and focus. They define whole peoples, attempting to silence the very voices that could awaken them. This very common form of bonding takes place when two or more people harass someone. Seeking this kind of agreement—this bonding with someone against someone else—is quite different from seeking validation.

Validation

Many abused people are afraid to talk to anyone about disturbing and painful events in their lives. They fear being accused by their abusers of "ganging up" with someone against them. "You are turning people against me" translates into "You are guilty and deserve my anger. Your pain is your fault." Or, in the workplace, the abused fear retaliation: They won't be believed. Their complaints will be dismissed. They will be made scapegoats for these or other problems. Or, they will be dismissed.

Even when Controllers wake from the spell and tell others of their misbehaviors, the listeners often find such revelations hard to accept. Recall Zee's words: "Everyone I've told, my family and friends, are incredulous. They've never seen this side of me!" Not only had they never seen this side of Zee, they had not even heard of it. Zee's wife, like many abused people, suffered a long time because she told no one. She didn't want to be accused by Zee of ganging up against him. And not knowing of the spell, nor even that she was in a verbally abusive relationship, she found no words to explain the inexplicable. She found no validation.

But just as we depend upon others for community and the exchange of ideas and information, we need someone to understand and validate our own experience, especially if it is very confusing. For instance, a Witness may ask a friend, "If this happened to you, what would you think?" Most people seek validation if they are defined or invalidated by someone over a period of time. In doing so, a person is not bonding together against someone. She is instead seeking assurance that her reality is real—in other words, that she's not crazy.

While validation is a confirmation of one's experience, getting agreement with someone to be against someone else or some group is quite different. Agreements between neighbors and nations can be all to the good if they support people and resist oppression. Agreements against others that are designed to control them are not. They deepen the spell.

Bonding Together Against Others

Diminishing and fighting against an authentic person or persons is something Controllers are used to doing, and when they convince someone else of their confabulations, or when they meet with no resistance, they feel that their "rightness" is confirmed. Pretend person or persons are alive and well and authentic person or persons are wrong, gone, or nonexistent. The more people agree with Controllers, the more certain and the more connected the Controllers feel.

There are many ways to bond together against others. Some people bond together with very large groups, such as one race or gender against another race or gender. If there are no persons of their race or gender present to bond with for this purpose, they do it in their imagination.

Here is an example. It happened to me and I was stunned.

I was on the phone exchanging information with a man known for his stance against domestic violence. I informed him of my work.

Suddenly he said, "Well, what do you want from us?"

"I don't think anything," I said, in answer to his unexpected question.

"Can't make up your mind, just like a woman," he said.

His response came as a complete surprise.

But suddenly, I knew a whole lot more about this man than I had known a moment before. In defining me he had pretended to be within me and so to know the nature of my mind and my decision-making processes. (In a certain sense he was "making up" my mind while telling me I couldn't make it up myself. This is pretty strange.) In his attempt to diminish my authentic self he had, in an imaginary way, also bonded with "men against women" (not all men, of course). Possibly he'd even pretended that by putting me down he'd put himself up. *Or perhaps he felt securely connected to dream women if authentic women could be so diminished.* I don't know. But, by seeing him from this perspective, I was much more able to understand why some women, who often hear this kind of denigration, begin to doubt themselves, even get caught in a deadly Control Connection.

I wondered if his professional advocacy of women threatened his sense of being a man. Had his father been consistently accepting, kind, nurturing? Did he feel a need to pull back from his declared alignment with a social cause to be more of a "real" man and hence to bond with men against women? These were only possibilities. What is important here is that bonding together against others can begin in the imagination but can materialize anywhere.

A man contacted me for a consultation after his wife had left him. He kept reiterating his beliefs that women want to be directed by men. Clearly, he was under the spell, defining half the species as if he were omniscient and, in doing so, bonding with imagined men who thought as he did. He told me much about himself. He felt directionless. Possibly he wanted to believe that his own need for inner direction matched a fabricated need in women for outer direction. Although making up women, especially in such an obvious way, seems silly, making up people can be dangerous. Out of such nonsense oppression thrives, wars are made, and relationships unmade.

The Spellbound person can bond together against others by finding another Spellbound person or group with whom to bond. We are all familiar with people who bond together against those who are different—people who are not the way the Spellbound want them to be—*the way they would be if they were their Pretend People.* Even the loner can do this in his or her imagination, with a me-against-them attitude. The man described by the press as the Unabomber, Theodore

Kaczynski, was such a loner. From the perspective of this book, he was extremely Spellbound. He was arrested in April 1996 and received three consecutive life sentences. He was accused of killing three people and injuring twenty-nine others with packaged mail bombs over almost two decades. Under the spell, he bonded together with a lot of people who resent the "evils" of technology *against* people who develop and work with technology. Then he carried out a personal vendetta against his victims—people who didn't think as he thought, act the way he wanted them to act, or be the Pretend People they *should* be.

He appeared to believe that if he were frightening enough, violent enough, and threatening enough he could make his dream world (a world without technology) be real.

Let's look at some hypothetical questions to illustrate how the Spellbound experience the threat of difference. Would the Spellbound bond together against those who are different if those who are different turned into *Pretend People*—people who had made themselves up "right"—people who appeared to be exactly like them? Would a white supremacist group bond together against an African-American group if the African-American group magically transformed into whites? Could people remain bonded together against people who appeared to be just like them? When Controllers act against those who are different, isn't it because they are both seeking to bond with each other and also angry that others are not as they "should" be?

Individuals who are Spellbound as well as groups who are Spellbound are surprisingly similar. A Controller might say, "You're looking for trouble, don't think you're going to get away with it." A street gang, bonded together against another gang, could say the same thing.

Bonding together against others is a sad and sick self-help program. With super-potent double connections, it relieves the nagging sting of disconnection, like cortisone on a rash. Each member of the group is connected to "The Group" and additionally to Pretend People, that is, the people the others "should" be. With collective agreement, such connections affirm the group's belief in their rightness and alleviate their identity dilemma, proclaim their superiority over those who are different, and assuage their fear of disconnection by "all-powerful" Spellbreakers.

Bonding together against others can happen anywhere. Albert told me the following story.

> *He was working in a busy marketing business. Twice a week he and four or five other staff members met to discuss various accounts and strategies. Shortly after he had acquired some large accounts and enjoyed some great success, the other staff members began to talk past him, not even glancing his way. When he contributed an idea or perspective, he was interrupted or received no response. He felt frustrated and uncertain. His attempts to be heard were futile.*

His colleagues showed no perception of him, *as if he were undefined and had no boundary at all,* as if he didn't exist.

They were threatened by his success, so they rid themselves of the threat. In this way they could remain immersed in their illusion: that if they had made themselves up right, *they* were successful—so he didn't exist.

Bonding together against others requires:

1. Being under the influence of the spell
2. Making one's self right and the other wrong
3. Finding another Spellbound person or group to bond with, be close to, or imagining one

4. Getting them to agree with you on who to make wrong—who to go against
5. Joining a group that has already made the selection for you

The Threat of Difference

When a deeply Spellbound Controller encounters someone with a very different worldview, especially someone from a different culture who assigns different meanings and values to everyday events, he faces many threats to his identity. He's made himself up right. How could anyone else be different *and* right? The threat of difference includes people of a different ethnicity, territory, culture, age, color, weight, length of residency, religion, lifestyle, occupation, sexual orientation, interest, political view, income, education, gender, diet, family origin, or any combination thereof. These differences are also signs of separateness.

Some groups form out of familial relationships: cousins, siblings, aunts, uncles, and so forth. These would normally be healthy groups, but, in some unusual cases, they can bond together against those who are not related to them. Nonfamily members are then considered outsiders.

> *Mira worked for a school district. Mira was different. She was not a sister, cousin, daughter, aunt, wife, in-law, or distant relative of the people in control in the district office, who had filled each new job opening, from teacher to aide, with a relative.*
>
> *She was given poor evaluations, ignored by peers in social situations, and reprimanded for other employees' mistakes. She had begun to suffer physical symptoms: anxiety, panic attacks, sleeplessness, and even rashes*

her doctor couldn't cure, and she was becoming exhausted. The stress of trying to be perfect to avoid further assaults, while not understanding why they occurred in the first place, had compromised her immune system.

I'd seen these symptoms before in many oppressive relationships. As we talked, Mira was able to see that her coworkers were bonded together against her, had made her their scapegoat, and were extremely superficial. Most of their energy went into looking good. They were for the most part disconnected and, she realized, they were unlikely to change.

With all of her wisdom, depth, and training, she also realized that she would do well on her own, consulting under contract. This she did. Her rashes, sleeplessness, and other health problems disappeared within a few days. She said that it was her understanding of Control Connections and the need of the Spellbound to bond together against others that gave her the confidence to make the change. As a consultant, she had so many opportunities she could pick and choose among them.

Without awareness, the Spellbound can sink ever more deeply into the spell. Always striving to dissolve all sense of disconnection, they may reinforce the spell among themselves by teaching their young who to be against.

When people are against other people *because* they are different from them, they don't explain their opposition by saying, "I am afraid of or feel threatened by people who are different from me." Instead they explain themselves with false reasons that are in fact confabulations that have been reinforced and passed on through generations until they have gained a certain acceptance.

In the same way that the husband in "The Corn Story"

raged at his authentic wife for displacing pretend wife, people who are against others don't really know why. Consequently, they make up a reason.

Generally, these "reasons" have *evolved* from singular confabulations to general "truths." And because they have existed in the culture or in the family for a long time, they are unquestioned. They seem like reality, like just the way it is. Prejudices and stereotypes are examples of evolved confabulations.

Prejudice

When people accept prejudice as truth, prejudice, like a battery, keeps them turned on and ready to go against others. But prejudice clouds vision and blocks awareness because it claims to know the reality of, or truth about, someone or some group without benefit of firsthand knowledge. When prejudice is against people, it devalues them.

Firsthand knowledge is concrete, like discovering a thief. Something is stolen and a person is found in possession of the stolen property. Even then a trial is required to determine if the evidence is adequate.

To illustrate the nonsensical quality of prejudice, I invite you to imagine walking into a children's daycare center and seeing ten three-year-old children, half female, half male, all of different height, ethnicity, weight, dexterity, and verbal skills. None is of more or less value than the other, but racial prejudice, gender prejudice, and other prejudices would say otherwise.

Stereotypes

The Spellbound support their prejudice with stereotypes. Stereotypes are illusions repeated in a culture until they are thought to be true. They "make up" people. They abound in movies, television shows, cartoons, comic strips, and many people's conversations. Racial, gender, and age stereotypes are common. Human disparagement, instead of being seen for what it is, becomes in some media a game, or clever repertoire. Unlike real life, the actors know it's only a game. After all, they're acting. Some people, however, in their real life accept the disparagement as a norm to be emulated.

Like a lens, a stereotype screens out reality, replacing it with an illusion that reinforces the spell, because the spell is, after all, a collection of illusions.

Some sayings, too, support prejudice and stereotypes. They masquerade as truth and dangerously carry the illusion of a collective authority behind them. "Curiosity killed the cat." "A woman's place is in the home." "It takes two." "Children are to be seen and not heard." These sayings oppose life and deepen the spell.

On the other hand, like a jewel in a simple setting, sayings can hold wisdom. "A stitch in times saves nine" is a saying that reveals the systemic principle: Something set in motion, if it is not stopped, will increase in intensity and frequency over time. A rip, for instance, will become a big rip.

Similarly, if a person connects backwards, making up a Pretend Person and anchoring it in the other (a rip in reality), doesn't then wake up and stop (mend it), he will continue trying harder and harder to prevent the other from showing signs of separateness. He will act more frequently and intensely until a final sign of separateness produces a final action resulting in a final separation (a big rip).

Others may have information that you don't have—for instance, your accountant. Others may be better able to predict the outcome of certain economic trends—for instance, your financial analyst. But, when it comes to knowing your inner experience, you are your own authority. An outside authority can only recommend, present a picture, offer an alternative, or ask.

When it comes to physical symptoms, an authority with specialized experience, such as a doctor, is more likely to discover and describe to you "what's wrong" than is the person who checks out your groceries. On the other hand, when someone like the woman who was told by her therapist to ignore her own intuition contacts me, I'm inclined to say, "Someone working at your grocery store may be more likely to understand your experience than the 'authority' you consulted." However, I do believe that therapy can greatly help people reconnect to themselves when they are willing to give up their connections to Pretend Persons. And I do recommend therapists who understand that when someone is trying to keep a Pretend Person anchored in a real person, the real person is not at fault.

Chapter XXIII

One Mind and the Conformity Connection

*Authenticity
is spellbreaking.*

A s we have seen, Pretend Person is always of one mind with the Controller. They're that close. They're that connected. And just as Controllers expect those people with whom they want to be close to conform to their mind, many Controllers also look for other people to be of one mind with them. One of the most certain ways to ensure one-mindedness is to bond together with others, not necessarily against someone or some group, but to bond together against change itself. Bonding together against change keeps a tight grip on the status quo, keeps things as they are.

Conformity, like glue, holds reality together for many people, and conformity connections appear as lifeboats in a sea of disconnection. They assure the group of their one-mindedness: that they are, indeed, connected. Even so, conformity connections are under constant attack. There are so many ways to rock the boat. Nonconformity, like authenticity, can appear at any moment, taking shape in new ideas, interests, careers, and lifestyles, threatening the group's grip on the status quo and, of course, their tenuous connections. Conformity connections perpetuate unawareness and deepen the spell. They thrive among those who have fallen under the spell, from families to dictatorships.

When the spell descends upon a family, bonding it together against change, conformity holds the family together, but in a backwards way. If family members, old enough to do so, do not share in decisions, in an atmosphere of mutuality, then no doubt a Controller rules with the threat of ostracism, disinheritance, rejection, or physical assault, among others. Conformity is requisite to the totalitarian authoritarianism that reigns in such families.

Conformity connections can also appear in the workplace. When conformity takes precedence over creativity, Controllers, who are already threatened by signs of separateness, will feel particularly threatened by nonconformity. Other people's thoughts, opinions, openness, and creativity oppose not only their Control Connections, but also their conformity connections. Consequently, people who express new thoughts and ideas may be ignored, scorned, made the object of hostility, or be told outright that they are expected to conform.

> *Richard, a high-tech professional employed almost twenty years by a large company, called to tell me he had just agreed to a transfer to a new location.*
>
> *He and his family traveled across country and hoped for the best.*
>
> *Not long after, he called to tell me that on his first day at work he was shocked to hear his manager say, "In this company conformance is more important than performance."*

The quality of his work and creativity had been acclaimed and were meaningful to him. Now it didn't seem to matter, at least not to the company. In a casual manner, as if it was normal, he had been told to maintain the status quo.

Richard paid a price for the freedom of authenticity. He left the company and started over, finding new employment and moving back across the country.

The stakes get even higher when a whole lot of people try to keep a grip on the status quo.

Galileo said, in essence, "We have it *backwards*. The sun doesn't go around the earth. The earth goes around the sun." Galileo's observations confirmed previous ones. But the prevailing authorities wanted Galileo to retract his observation because he was not of one mind with them. They were Spellbound. They not only made up people—how they should be and what they should do and what was "wrong with them"—but also made up the universe and how it is and what it does. In an illusory way they were bonded together with God (as they imagined God) against Galileo.

They were reluctant to allow a new idea "in," because it would threaten their identities as authorities, their conformity connections, and their bond with each other and God in a seeming pact against those who were of a different mind.

Galileo wasn't willing to conform. Consequently, he was tried by Inquisition and forced to recant. He died nine years after the ordeal. His idea had threatened to loosen the authorities' grip on the status quo, so they thought it opposed God.

Wherever people claim to be privy to God, the spell is likely at work.

In our time Galileo might have put his new idea on the Internet. Arresting him wouldn't have stopped the idea even temporarily because in a moment or so just about everybody would have known. Keeping a grip on the status quo isn't as easy as it once was, because now there are an ever-growing number of new ideas, innovations, and world views to oppose, all proliferating in cyberspace, threatening conformity connections wherever they exist.

In retaliation, leaders in some countries have bonded together against Internet access to respected journals and newspapers. In Myanmar (formerly called Burma) the Internet is outlawed.[6] And in Afghanistan even computers are confiscated.[7] Just the *idea* of people having instant access to news and views that don't conform to their "let's pretend" world threatens Controllers.

The most dramatic demonstrations of conformity connections appear in "mob mentality" and "cult compliance." These territories demonstrate the power of the compelling force in situations where it is least understood and most opposed.

Mob Mentality

When a crowd is led off purpose, it is almost always against others. The conformity connection is most concisely evident in its instant form, mob mentality—a demonstrator fends off an attack, a protest becomes a riot.

Nowhere is conformity more quickly established than in mob mentality, and seldom is it more obvious than in the strange phenomenon of mob violence. The spell can settle on the unsuspecting with little resistance. The one-mindedness of mob mentality, expressed in violence, offers a seemingly instant cure for disconnection. It seduces not only with the promise of instant connection, but also with the collective agreement of "rightness."

A catalyst is all that's required. When one person breaks a window or throws a rock, people with a me-against-them mentality are inclined to join in and a riot can ensue. Similarly, violence between groups can break out. One person jostles another. Someone pushes back. Someone is dark-skinned. Someone is light-skinned. Someone is uniformed and someone is not. Doesn't matter. In an instant, *difference* is perceived and the spell has its way.

We've seen how people with prejudicial ignorance bond together against others in loosely organized or unplanned ways. Now, before we explore how people bond together against others in a highly organized manner, we will take a look at a most extraordinary kind of bonding: people who, in a highly organized way, are bonded together, not necessarily against others, but against themselves and for their leader.

The Cult: A Triple Connection

The most highly organized, completely pretend world is that of the cult. The cult leader, the primary Controller, makes up everything relevant to the meaning, purpose, and function of the cult, as well as to the members' lives. He has the final say in all decisions, even personal ones. In effect the leader becomes the members' "self," as was Marshall Applewhite of the infamous Heaven's Gate cult. Under Applewhite's direction, cult members joined him in committing suicide en masse.

Applewhite, like all cult leaders, established a Control Connection to his followers. They were his Pretend People. He knew how they should be, and he experienced ongoing "proof" of his rightness, because he was followed even into death.

As cultists become disconnected from themselves, they are coerced into connecting to a pretend *self*, the leader. In other words, as one's self is lost, the leader becomes it. In order to maintain a position of total control, the leader enforces strict conformity and often manipulates members into enforcing compliance among themselves.

The leader, like the Controllers we have met thus far, defines others: he or she "knows" who and what the others should be and what they should do, and rules like a god. Cultists eventually find inner or self-direction to be almost impossible.

When a former member and sole survivor of the Heaven's Gate cult suicides was asked if he intended to lead others into a cult, he said, "We can't even lead ourselves."[8]

Like the interlocking pieces of a picture puzzle, the leader and the cult members fit together to form a complete picture. But this picture is not a visual one. It is instead a psychological one: a Control Connection of the greatest magnitude.

Full-fledged cult members may become Controllers on behalf of the leader. To coerce new members, they whittle, belittle, degrade, attack, demote, demean, and attempt to seriously undermine the very fabric of the other's reality. They usually do this not intending to destroy the other, but intending to turn the other into a Pretend Person—a person of one mind with them, able to enter into a pretend world with them.

After a while, cult candidates lose their self-connection in systematic conditioning. Not unlike severely abused children and people in severely abusive relationships, their communication is controlled or under rigid constraints. They are watched for signs of separateness and punished for them. They are relentlessly coerced to become Pretend People, designed to inhabit a pretend world imagined by their leader.

If cultists are successful, cult candidates will doubt themselves and open up to indoctrination. In fact, if their belief systems and personal realities are shattered, the cult, and particularly their leader, will seem to bring salvation. The cult reality, a newly fabricated belief system, then replaces personal reality. Cults are formed by this process. New members must be convinced of their "wrongs," so that their leader, an abuser of power, can "lead them to redemption" along prescribed lines of conduct.

Through indoctrination, brainwashing and ever-increasing pressure from members, cult candidates shift from tenuous self-connection to solid cult connection. They are finally *triply* connected: connected with each other against themselves, connected to their leader, and connected in conformity to one mind.

I was afforded an extraordinary opportunity to interview a woman who left a cult when in her mid-twenties. Her remarkable strength touched and inspired me. She had made meaning of her horrifying experience and had found a purpose in her life. As she related her story to me, I understood as never before how the Controller's grip in a person's mind is a constant assault on her reality.

The following is developed from this interview. Please note that a cult leader may be male or female but in this case was male.

The cult leader appears to have special knowledge—knowledge that no one else could have. He is certain of this. His knowledge comes from beyond the world, from Christ, God, or a being from another planet or time. It is as if his knowledge is backed by a myth that has now become real. Others are told that only with this knowledge will they be saved. He alone can save them. He alone knows what they should do, how they should be, how they are, and what they are. He does not doubt himself. Convinced and convincing, he brings the cult into existence.

Isolation is a major factor. Cultists don't know that they are living in a "pretend world." They are allowed little or no contact outside the cult, or they are taught to fear "outsiders." They have no frame of reference, no contrast to enable them to make the distinction between the world we all live in and the cult's world. It is imperative that all follow the leader's direction or they will suffer unspeakable loss: to be cast out of the "world," where there is no protection from the "evil" he is saving them from.

The rules are terribly strict. Members may live in their own homes, but their dress, budget, and activities are all subject to the leader's approval. They are isolated not only from the outside world, but also from each other. They are taught that they have no access to truth.

An exception to this is a kind of cult that teaches that truth will come in some strange way, apart from all reason. These cults lead their members so deeply into their past memories that the feelings these memories generate leave them powerless and unable to function in the present. Hence they are subject to the leader's control.

Generally, cult members must reveal all their thoughts to their leader and so are made to betray their basic loyalties. These secret revelations are used as special knowledge to further exalt the leader. No one has a confidant. Members' mail and journals are monitored. Their conversations are subject to scrutiny. Usually, privacy is forbidden. The leader can walk into any home, any bedroom, any place a member may be, and his invasion is accepted because his "contact" has authorized it.

The leader steps into the minds of the members with the authority of a god. He claims secret knowledge and plays upon any information he gleans from other members. He appears all-knowing.

Paradoxically, no cult members recognize that the group is a cult. The members feel that they are the chosen ones. Insiders. Privy to secret and life-saving knowledge—knowledge that comes from the "beyond" through their leader.

Following are excerpts from an interview with the former cult member mentioned previously:

> *The cult leader relentlessly breaks down all boundaries surrounding the psyches of his followers . . .*
>
> *We were not allowed to show any feelings, to have any knowing of anything from within ourselves . . .*
>
> *We were not allowed to say no. It was not possible to say no. A child could be secretly and awfully punished for saying no. We would be beaten . . .*
>
> *We were conditioned to look outside of ourselves for direction, knowledge, safety . . .*
>
> *We lived in a spiritual prison. But we were told that if we followed every rule, we would be most spiritual . . .*
>
> *We had no human validation and little access to truth . . .*
>
> *We had to be perfect. We could not experiment and risk failure . . .*
>
> *If we did something judged as wrong, we faced rage . . .*

There was a lot of blaming and anger pointed at the other . . .

He so craftily demeaned what I later discovered was my true talent, I believed I was unable to live in the outside world. That there was nothing I could do. That I would die. Now, many years later, with anguish I fully realize the depth of his deceit.

To leave the cult was to leave my family and all that I knew.

"How did you do that?" I asked.
She replied:

I took their beliefs and carried them through to the farthest extreme and proved to myself they made no sense. They also had many beliefs that could neither be proven nor disproved.

I snuck out at night and sat in the dark in nature and had a sense of unity with something real.

And, my instincts seemed to be reliable and took me this way.

When I was quite young I started keeping a journal. Of course they read it. They started to see my thoughts didn't conform. In the end I was given an ultimatum. And around that time, another member shared a terrible secret with me, that the leader had assaulted her sexually. I told her I believed her. It had happened more than once to me, on Saturday nights.

Then on Sunday morning to hear him preaching and being god could not fit with that other knowledge. I'd split it off within myself. I'd had no memory 'till she said it.

*In one way I left and in another way my world
ended. My parents and family were no longer available
to me. I'd been born into the cult.*

On recovery:

*It takes a long, long time. The process unfolds at
its own pace. I could not rush it. The arts are very, very
helpful.*
*I did not know I had my talent till I had a flash-
back and felt the anguish of being told I had none.
That pronouncement had devastated me. I cried
buckets.*
Practicing my art is most healing.
I read almost endlessly.
I write.
*I attend Adult Children of Alcoholics. ACA helps
a lot.*

As we have seen, conformity connections show up in many
ways. Controllers attempt to control others by being part of a
mob acting against others, or by being bonded with others
against new ideas, or by coercing new or potential cult members, or even by being a cult leader—an ultimate Controller. It
seems that Controllers feel so compelled to control, that one
way or another they will find a way to exert pressure, if not pain,
on others. The further we look, the more places Controllers
seem to show up. Are their needs and their numbers so great
that their controlling behaviors have been normalized, at least in
some instances? We'll explore this idea in the next chapter.

Chapter XXIV

Control: Perpetuated and Institutionalized

In a "let's-pretend" world,
it is no wonder there is war.

We have explored the spell and disconnection, found Control Connections to be sick substitutes for the real thing, and discovered people bonding together against others in mobs, in conformity, and in cults—wherever two or more people are gathered together against the other.

In order to find the compelling force behind oppressive behaviors, we will travel through some territories where the spell reigns supreme. We'll see how Control Connections are institutionalized and even in some places normalized until they're called tradition—such as Afghanistan.

Gangs, criminal cartels, dictatorships, military regimes, hate groups, and terrorist organizations are examples of groups bonded together against others. The bond itself is a powerful opiate. The belief that members of the group are superior to others enhances each member's feeling of being connected, of being close, accepted, and secure.

People seeking this bond are easy prey to leaders who would use them, mobilize them, and build a force from them for their own purposes: to acquire the resources and labor of others, to make themselves right, and to control or to annihilate the other. The very act of attempting to have power over another person makes the other the enemy.

To assure their survival, these groups demand allegiance. Members must stand together even when the group's actions go against their deepest values. "I was only taking orders." Allegiance demands conformance. Being of one mind assures it.

Groups organized against others define those whom they've bonded together against as inferior or as outsiders or as not fully human. As they define the other, they become Pretenders. And because they are able to suppress their knowledge of the common humanity of all people, they become devoid of conscience. Some exploit others and institutionalize their "make believe" by establishing class systems, castes, and hierarchies. These oppressive systems are so pervasive and long-standing that Controllers call them traditions.

Gangs

Gangs are small groups bonded together against others. Gang members, Spellbound from childhood, defined and developed backwards, form gangs to alleviate their feelings of disconnection. Their compliance to gang rules confirms and reinforces their bonds and their one-mind connection.

They prove their allegiance and conformity by their willingness to act against others. The others are often members of another gang.

The difference between two gangs can be as slight as whether the members are newly immigrated or not, or even as slight as the difference between living on one side of the street or the other. Although difference can be almost anything, by establishing "those who are different" and "those who are us," gang members feel connected to each other.

In some groups, once difference is perceived and the gang is formed, they choose their color. For instance, one gang may wear red, another green. To either group the one that is different is the enemy and wrong and easily identifiable. The members are of one mind. They all agree that they are right. Their identity is affirmed by their position in the gang, and the pain and anxiety of their disconnection is temporarily relieved.

Gangs are like hate groups but their prejudice is barely articulated. For the most part, they need only be able to discern the difference between one color and another. They rely on colors and territory and who has what, as well as who has what they want, to help them see whom to be against. They would not be against anyone who transformed into the person they "should" be, for instance, a member of their gang.

Hate Groups

Hate groups are also bonded together against real people. They are like gangs but are usually more organized. Generally their cause is well articulated. Let's look at a hate group's position through the lens of this book.

They are angry that anyone different from them would dare consider themselves equal. They've made themselves up right and superior. Just the existence of "those people" acting equal is an attack on the hate group members' identities as well as their connections to the pretend people the others "should be." If only everyone would be just like them.

They know how you should be, and if you are different in some particular way, they hate you. They are bonded together in their hate and they are sure they're right because they are of one mind. They are righteous, acceptable, superior, and last but not least, close and connected (backwards).

Members of terrorist organizations, like those of hate groups, are connected to the world backwards. And when the real world displaces their pretend worlds, what else is there to do but bring destruction to make it go away? Locked into Control Connections and anchored in a pretend world they engage in a terrorist lifestyle, terrorizing and even killing the "enemy."

Extreme Control

Can you imagine driving down a street and being suddenly pulled from your car by an angry mob? Can you imagine the terror of knowing that you are being beaten to death? This happened to a woman in Afghanistan in the 1990s. Ostensibly because her arm was accidentally seen. Accidentally uncovered.

Thousands like her languish in a kind of prison, hidden away within cloth cages, garments that cover them completely. They have only tiny slits to see through and hardly space to move their arms. Some 35,000 of them, because they are widows and have no man to provide for them, go hungry and see their children go hungry. Doctors, educators, professionals, and other workers, who just like us worked daily at their jobs, and who just like us were so liberated they could keep their own names when they married, are forbidden employment and freedom. They are told it is because they are female.

Their oppressors are the Taliban of Afghanistan, an extremist Islamic group that appears to be one of the most cowardly and most organized of all groups bonded together against others.

Collectively, the men of the Taliban are connected backwards to women and to the feminine. Through cultural mores, countless wars, and military training, they have lost connection to themselves. They are deeply Spellbound. They are afraid to stand alone. They anchor in the collective woman. They hide their cowardly acts, not behind their mothers' skirts, but behind God and tradition.

To protect themselves from their fear of women's authenticity, they avoid signs of women's separateness in an appalling way. They make women as invisible and nondescript as possible. Backed by the country's militia, they hide authentic women within cloth cages, threatening them with death if they show signs of separateness. And they don't hesitate to kill. Just as a woman was dragged from her car and stoned to death, other women have been killed for independent acts.

When an authentic woman can't be seen at all, it is easier for the Controller to keep pretending. When she is in a cloth cage, there are no signs of separateness to break the spell. The Controller can hide from his own cowardice, his fear of standing alone, separate from her.

While the men of the Taliban control with force and threats, the women suffer a living death. Escape from their home to their yard, if they are not under the surveillance of a male and in a cloth cage, invites a horrible death. The Controllers make certain that in no way will Teddy get away, nor will anyone see her.

Every effort is made to disconnect these women from their minds and bodies. Girls are forbidden education, although some get enough before the age of nine to read the rules. All this because they are female and because they are real people.

Their difference and authenticity are threatening. As always the Taliban's bonds to dream woman and to each other offer a double connection and collective consensus. The Taliban "know" they are right because they've made themselves up to be right and they "know" that God is on their side.

Clearly, hiding authentic women makes it easier to keep pretend women "alive." So terrified is the Taliban male of losing the body that anchors his Teddy that he can neither hear nor see the real person who inhabits it. And the real person is forbidden even to wear shoes that could make noise while she walks. Also horrifying is the fact that people born in cages are likely to eventually find it natural to stay there.

Imagine, if you would, a Controller coming home and seeing only a shadow. How easily the Taliban male fills it with dream woman's form. Imagine coming home and hearing only silence. How easy to imagine what one wants. No real woman to distract from Pretend Person, to break the spell, to shatter the illusion—an illusion as infantile as the illusion of an all-need-meeting mother.

The Taliban's terrible gender apartheid was firmly established in the fall of 1996 when they took over Kabul, the capital of Afghanistan. The outcome of all the restrictions is starvation, trauma, depression, and death.

In August 1998, *The Journal of the American Medical Association* reported that of 160 Afghanistan women surveyed,

97 percent showed evidence of major depression. Eighty-six percent had significant anxiety symptoms. (Half the women were living in Afghanistan's capital and half were from Afghanistan and had recently migrated to Pakistan.)

The Taliban hide their need to control real women under the guise of Islamic religion, as if their cowardly and cruel actions were actually religious. However, mainstream Islamic peoples do not condone the Taliban's control tactics.

In the United States and most countries where men and women are equally horrified by the holocaustal portent of this imprisonment, the power of the spell can never be taken lightly. There are legions of men, albeit unorganized and scattered throughout the world, who have stood in front of a door blocking a woman's escape, who have pulled a phone from the wall or taken the car keys to keep her from getting help, who have threatened to take her children if she tried to get away, who have told her who and what she is and what she must do, who have kept her from gainful employment, who have threatened to break her bones or bruise her body or have done so, who have threatened to kill her or who have done so. All the while believing they loved her too much.

Bonding Together Against Children

Unconscious and seemingly benign Control Connections such as Betty had with her daughter, taken to the extreme, lead us to another dark area in our journey of exploration through the maze of senseless behaviors woven into our world. This is the forcing of real children to be pretend children. It is another massive assault upon humanity that takes place where adults are bonded together against millions of real children. The real children are replaced by pretend children born in the minds of Controllers to work like slaves.

Can you imagine working from dawn well into dark, all the while hungry and exhausted, cringing to avoid frequent random blows, separated from family and living in squalid conditions? Can you imagine trying to stay alive in a dark factory or a hot field, where all your childhood is erased by people who hold power over you?

The Controllers who perpetuate this slave labor aren't restrained by the horror of what they are doing because they have made up pretend children who are meant to do their bidding. They don't hate real children, rather they don't "see" them as real people. They only see their pretend children.

Millions of boys and girls are forced into slave labor, working long hours in horrifying conditions. They are bought, sold, and beaten, and some are raped.

Sometimes they are brainwashed to believe that entering into this labor is a normal step toward adulthood. Similarly, in the time of slavery in America, the persons enslaved were told how glad they should feel that they had their place in God's plan, that God had shown them their role in society.

Many of the children who are now enslaved begin labor at three or four years of age. About half are under the age of ten. This is happening in Pakistan, China, India, Indonesia, and other countries. This happens wherever Controllers are too cowardly to stand on their own two feet, without the support of a child. The spell feeds their greed.[9]

Some groups are so deeply Spellbound that they bond together to wage war to avenge confabulated or ancient wrongs, or simply to get rid of Spellbreakers. They reinforce their rationale among themselves, gain as much agreement as possible, become of one mind, stay connected.

They may call their wars "religious" and claim God is on their side. To make this claim, they form a backwards connection to God. They do this in the same way that we have seen people forge backwards connections to others, to be "close."

To connect to God backwards, the group first makes up a pretend God who agrees with them, one that only they are privy to. They then come to believe that their pretend God is God. They're "so close" that they know what God wants, thinks, and feels, and what God expects of one. And, most significant, they know whose side God is on. Theirs. Thus they "know" that God is "unhappy" with those who are not of one mind with them.

After arranging to have God on their side, they make up Pretend People who believe as they believe, think as they think, and do what they "should." They then go about trying to replace authentic people with their Pretend People. When they meet with resistance, they become ever more oppressive, righteous, and vociferous. Eventually they kill the people they are bonded together against and call it a "religious" war. "Religious" wars are about bonding together against others to avoid disconnection. They are designed to rid the world of Spellbreakers. All other "reasons" are confabulated to make such senseless behavior seem sensible, to make the aggression seem reasonable.

Perpetrators hide behind the ideologies of church or state or tradition or ancient wrongs to disguise and justify being bonded together against others.

What, seemingly, can be more powerful than en masse allegiance for a cause, and more certain than a world of like-mindedness ensuing from the destruction of all perceived opposition? With this bonding people no longer need be uncertain, separate, free, and autonomous, nor have they need to explore their purpose and meaning. They are embraced within a system that personifies their "truth."

Throughout history, these power structures that seemed to ensure survival have struggled for their own survival. Rising and collapsing on false foundations and taking lives with them, religious wars, ethnic "cleansing," genocides, inquisitions, and persecutions are all manifestations of Control Connections formed to keep the fear of disconnection at bay, formed in service to a leader who is the authority on such matters. Mass murders of ethnic Albanians in Kosovo are a recent example.

But religion and tradition are not about war. Ancient mythologies, antique religions, as well as contemporary ones, emerged to support people's lives, to alleviate suffering, and to express connection to All That Is, by whatever name: God, Goddess, the Messiah, the Supreme Being, the Great Spirit, Jevah, Brahman, Nirvana, or Allah.

Rituals and practices have also emerged that, like prescriptions, treat the symptoms of disconnection, the feeling of being lost or beside oneself in order to bring awareness of true connection, the feeling of being found, connected within, i.e., inner-connected. Since most of us have felt lost, beside ourselves, or disconnected at some time, they support us on our life journey.

But to the severely disconnected, the person whose identity is built backwards, everything, not to mention eternity, hangs on his or her having the right prescription—the right dogma. Since the person's identity is constructed primarily from beliefs *about* reality, any other nonconforming belief system challenges his or her very being. As if they *are* their ideologies, Controllers think differing ideas and views are personal opposition to be rejected and destroyed. And, since Controllers identify themselves with their prescriptions, it becomes important to them that others be dissuaded of theirs. Their success is measured in conversions.

Paradoxically, the fear of separateness, of difference, of being found out and finding themselves out, prevents deeply Spellbound people from the very religious experience that could alleviate their fears.

Additionally, some people under the guise of religion *teach* backwards connections. They do not embrace the real meaning of religion. Carl Gustav Jung stated that the word "religion" is derived from the word *religere,* which means to reconnect through recollection—a turning inward. But rather than leading others to build their spiritual connections from the inside out, some Spellbound people mandate a human authority to build a false connection from the outside in. Quite the opposite of life as we know it.

Dogmas and practices that arise out of backwards connections foster the very disconnection they are meant to heal. In this sense, do the Spellbound know what they do?

Why would it matter to anyone what anyone else believed, said, or did, as long as it was not harmful to other people? Can there be anything more harmful than going against people who were different or who believed, thought, or did *differently?*

In contradistinction to the perpetuation and institutionalization of control, most people strive to live harmoniously with each other and with nature. The lives of millions of people over millennia testify to the fact that many people bond together *for,* rather than against, others. They form charitable institutions, volunteer organizations, and support groups to assist others. Their bonds empower them to express truth, mutuality, and love itself.

Part IV

We have explored the spell and its many dimensions, seen how it can descend upon an individual and how, just as readily, it can descend upon a group. We've found that people who fall under the spell's influence rarely realize it and may even have good intentions.

No matter who they are, most people who have taken on a controlling lifestyle are shocked when they realize it. They find it very difficult to get out from under the spell even when they very much want to change, even when they want to preserve a relationship or to stay out of jail. What holds them back?

We'll enter some new territory to find some answers. In the next chapters we'll discover the compelling force and take a look at real connections. We'll confront the last strange paradox. Then we'll move on to explore "Breaking the Spell." Our journey will end, in the last chapter, when we'll see what it's like to live aligned with the compelling force.

Chapter XXV

The Compelling Force

*The compelling force is
so powerful, inexorable,
and eternal that it
cannot be ignored.*

While we long for an end to poverty and oppression, or greater spirituality, stronger families, safer streets, or a healthy environment, are we not, in our hearts, longing for clarity—an understanding of what compels the chaos?

Although we have hundreds of explanations for violence, abuses, cults, gangs, "religious" wars, and atrocities, we seem not to have a clear perception of why they happen, that is, what is at their core. Most of us strive to be our best, but the very fact that our best has not brought forth the kind of world we would like suggests to me that there is a force we have neither seen nor taken into account.

If we do take *it* into account, I believe that we cannot help but bring into existence a safer and saner world.

Of course, because they are Spellbound, people who attempt to control others do not understand what compels them. When blaming others is no longer an option, and they awaken to their oppressive behavior, they are at a loss to explain themselves.

> *I realize that the wreck I am in is all my own doing. For too long I've clung to the belief that my bad behaviors would stop if only she would do/wouldn't do . . . (whatever).*
>
> *—G.L.*

Like Zee, whom we met earlier, G.L. realized that his oppressive behaviors had made a "wreck" of his life, but he was bewildered and, like Zee, he wanted to know, "What compels me to act like that?"

If there is a compelling force, what is it?

We are familiar with some forces. They run through us like energy. For example, we experience creative, emotional, and social forces because we are creative, emotional, and social beings. Let's briefly explore them so that when we come upon the compelling force, we'll see it very clearly.

First the creative force: Needing to experience our creativity, we feel compelled to use the creative force to bring into the world everything from an engaging mystery book to a majestic spacecraft, from a handmade greeting card to science, art, institutions, and families. Since we are already creative, creating is what we do. The creative force compels us to create. We consciously use this force when we set the stage for inspiration and use its energy to bring our ideas to fruition.

But even this force can be turned *backwards*. Why would such a great force—energy that arises from within, that compels creation and participation in life—be given over to disintegration and destruction? We'll find out soon. But first let's look at the two other forces—emotional and social.

The emotional force, like the creative force, is compelling. We grieve in times of loss, radiate joy when we've overcome a great adversity, and pursue our interests with passion. Emotion empowers our work, influences our choices, and helps us to make meaning of our experience. Emotion fuels our determination to stand for justice, speak out against oppression, solve our problems. Emotion colors our lives and renders possible our deepest understanding of the human condition. But even emotional force can be turned *backwards*. This great force, an energy that arises from within, that compels creation and participation in life, can be abdicated to indifference, hostility, and hate.

Last, we look at the social force. We are social beings. From the dawn of our species, we have participated in a social milieu. In ages past, we formed clans and tribes to survive the wilds. Now we build organizations and institutions to enhance the quality of life.

We are compelled to experience contact with others. Even

an infant whose needs for food and warmth are well met cannot survive without contact. The child who cannot reach out must be reached out to or it will die, so great is its need to experience the other.

But the need for social contact can also be turned *backwards*. This great force, an energy that arises from within that compels creation and participation in life, can be frozen in the cold depths of silence, isolation, and even paranoia.

If some people destroy rather than create, rage rather than feel, isolate rather than relate, then clearly they are responding to a compelling force. What great force, *when unattended*, turns back the creative, emotional, and social forces?

Just as we are already creative, emotional, and social beings, we are also *already* connected. And, just as we are compelled to experience our creative, emotional, and social nature, we are compelled to experience our connectedness.

Clearly, the compelling force is human consciousness itself seeking to know and to experience its own connectedness. This understanding is of profound consequence in our daily lives.

So powerful is this need that people who are unable to experience their own connectedness, both to self and others, commonly meet this need by creating a counterfeit connection to a Pretend Person, a pretend group, or a pretend world.

It is only when people's connection to self is lost or impaired and they are unable to connect through empathy to others that they connect in this illusory way. This illusory way of connecting brings about Control Connections, and Control Connections are just the opposite of empathetic ones and just the opposite of true connections. They drive others away.

Let us now look at how people under the influence of the compelling force seek connection. This excursion will serve also as a review before we go on to look at true connection and true separateness.

When people are disconnected from themselves, whether due to trauma, family or cultural influences, drug use, or all of these, they are "beside" themselves. But they have a compelling need to feel connected both to themselves and to others. If they try to meet their need in an unconscious way by first connecting to an illusion instead of themselves, then anchoring their illusion within real people or groups, their need for connection is not met. So they try to preserve their illusory connection. Thus they become Controllers.

In personal relationships, a Controller's efforts to keep up the illusion can escalate to verbal or physical abuse, betrayals, violence, and sometimes murder. Being connected to, or being made the object of this connection in this way, is mind-boggling and terrifying.

In ignorance, Controllers take up residence within Witnesses, as if they lived there and were privy to the Witnesses' inner realities. Without knowledge of the compelling force or of the possibility of real connection, Controllers feel constantly threatened by the Witnesses' separateness. As they defend their "position," their words take on a horrifying quality that thousands of people have told me is worse than physical blows.

- "You're trying to get out of it."
- "You're looking for trouble."
- "You don't know when to let well enough alone."
- "You really like doing this work."

When Controllers enter another person's reality this way, they feel so connected, so re-anchored and right, that they don't notice the other's separateness, nor do they realize the impact of their own behavior. But almost everyone I have spoken to has said that being the object of a Control Connection leaves them feeling disintegrated, as if they were being dismantled within.

By criticizing or diminishing even one small choice, one little belief, one opinion, or one feeling of the other, the Controller, knowingly or unknowingly, may have begun the dismantling process.

If a Controller succeeds in defining the real person, that person loses at least some self-awareness, hence some of their freedom. If people base their choices on what they've been *told* rather than on their own experience, a lifetime of difficulty may ensue. When people lose their sense of self, their identity is shaped by the confabulations they hear. "I guess I'm too sensitive. What's wrong with me?"

When the spell is at work, the well-intentioned often do not know what has come over them, yet neither do the Witnesses. In one-to-one relationships, the outcome of oppressive behaviors is horrifying. It is one thing to define a person and another to blow up a building in an act of terrorism, but both oppressive behaviors originate with the Controller's irrational "let's pretend" approach, just an attempt to feel connected.

Trying to be seen and heard, experiencing jolts and shocks to their psyches, Witnesses suffer from trauma complicated by post-traumatic stress.

Even when people don't allow another person to define them, if they don't understand the nature of control and the compelling force behind Control Connections, they sometimes spend their lives trying either to get the Controller to change or to prove that they're *not* what they've been told, not as they have been characterized: that what they've heard about themselves is not true.

For example, a woman harassed at work stayed on the job to gain respect and to prove she didn't deserve the abuse. She left only when she could no longer bear not being treated as a human being. By that time, no one believed she'd been harassed. If she had been, "Why did she stay so long?" they asked.

No one can prove themselves to a Controller. These efforts alone do not break the spell. In fact, the more authentic and strong Witnesses become, the more Controllers feel threatened and so escalate the attacks that tighten their grip.

Clearly, control isn't just about getting someone to do something. It's about the Spellbound fighting to avoid feeling adrift—disconnected in everyday life. Just as people who encounter Controllers are often surprised to find out why people would want to control them, so, too, Controllers are surprised to discover the kinds of illusions they've been living under as well as the fear they've kept at bay with their backwards connections.

At the most extreme, Controllers attempt to rid the world of those who are not as they "should be," not like their pretend people. Hitler is a perfect example of this extreme. In childhood he was disconnected from himself by horrific abuse.[10]

When people make up a pretend world, one without "different" people, for instance, and hook other people into their pretend world, as Hitler did, they can exert power over many. They can start a war.

Some people move in and out of the spell (they are far from the extreme). When they are living under extraordinary stress or suffer from a chemical imbalance, they may suddenly be beside themselves. If they can't seem to get a grip within themselves, they may try to get a grip within the other by defining them. But because they are not so deeply immersed in the spell that they cannot hear the other, they listen when their behavior is pointed out to them. They apologize and seek whatever help they need. Sometimes they only need a reminder that the spell is descending.

Understanding the compelling force, that is, the need to experience their own connectedness, offers the Spellbound an opportunity to consciously choose to stop pretending.

Chapter XXVI

True Connection

*Simply put, feeling connected
is perceiving ourselves as a
meaningful part of all.*

Knowing that we are all interconnected in a real but mysterious way is essential. We are connected to each other in our humanity and connected to the world around us because we are all a part of nature. Such knowledge helps Controllers to let go of Control Connections. Even when they feel adrift, disconnected from *themselves*, if they know that they are, in fact, connected to all, their fear and anxiety is lessened.

Also, such knowledge helps Witnesses to stand up to psychic assaults: *I have a right to be here. I am part of the universe. I cannot be erased.* Knowing about our interconnectedness is also essential if we are to fully understand what control is about.

An empathetic connection is the means by which we naturally experience our interconnectedness. Empathy flows from one person to another and arises out of our already being connected. Even children, unless they are beside themselves, experience empathy demonstrably by the age of two.[11]

Although we hear of our interconnectedness in popular literature, from the field of systems theory to the works of Deepak Chopra, we have not attended to the harm that arises from an ignorance of this knowledge.

I've spoken with many people who desperately wanted to give up their illusions and to learn to relate honestly and kindly to others, especially to those closest to them. Although fear and the memory of failed attempts stood in the way, a conceptual awareness, at least, of their interconnectedness, helped them to give up their Control Connections, to let go of their grip within the other, and to entertain the idea that, just maybe, they wouldn't die.

When Controllers face their fears and feelings, they can begin to connect within. When we are connected within, we know what we are experiencing. We know our feelings, sensations, and intuitions, and we are able to evaluate and integrate them. We make meaning of them. We have no need to connect to an illusion.

People who know their inner worlds feel connected to themselves—experiencing their *inner*-connectedness. And they then feel their connection to others—experiencing their *inter*connectedness. Consequently, they don't depend on Control Connections to keep themselves anchored. They are anchored within.

One of the reasons it has been difficult for some people to experience their inner-connectedness is that western culture not only has been outwardly focused to the exclusion of inner experience, but also has adopted a philosophy of duality. This philosophy assumes that the power and grace of the universe, of All That Is, is something so separate that when we say God, we already mean that which is separate from us, as if we were not held in divine intention—a part of all that is. This duality, like a mindset, can act as a lens excluding the experience of connectedness.

Rather than recognizing that they are a part of all and therefore already connected to that which is greater, some people have been influenced to place the "Great All" outside of themselves. They've imagined a man, "God," or a woman, "Goddess," and instead of seeing the image as representing All That Is, or even the very finest of that which is within each of us, they have attempted to resolve the dichotomy by becoming pleasing to that which is beyond them. In this way they have removed themselves from the nature of their existence, their connectedness, hence the wonder of their being.

Contemplation of the mystery of the human spirit, indeed of the universe itself, allows for the possibility that the divine permeates and sustains us and every atom of our being. Recall the woman who found the strength to leave the cult she had been born into: "I . . . sat in the dark in nature and had a sense of unity with something real."

Since establishing Control Connections and bonding together against others are common but sad substitutes for the real thing—a sense of connectedness—let's explore some of the ways in which we can realize our interconnectedness. One of the most common is a natural experience of unity.

People are increasingly reporting what is best described as a "unity experience," that is, perceiving the world as so "real" that they actually experience oneness with it. Renowned psychologist Abraham Maslow described many of these experiences.[12] People reported that when having such an experience their perception of the world suddenly changed. It seemed to become them and they *It*. They felt at one with all.

I asked four friends, "Have you ever had an experience of being at one with the world?" Without hesitation all four said "yes." Some had experienced this several times. They described their experiences similarly, as unforgettable—a deep feeling of peace, rightness, and timelessness. They felt secure. One man described his perception of oneness as occurring over a period of many days while a timeless present permeated his awareness.

Different traditions describe this experience in different ways: a moment of amazing grace, a transformative experience, an enlightenment, and so on.

Many people find that the practice of journal writing—a few minutes a day spent in getting in touch with one's self—can give rise to a sense of unity with all. Perhaps such practices are as important as their advocates say they are, especially considering the consequences of disconnection.

We can also understand our interconnectedness by looking at the origins of religions built around this knowledge. The original meaning of religion, to turn inward, suggests a way to remember our interconnectedness by experiencing it from within. Our connection to all is also verified by the cultures of a variety of indigenous populations, such as Native Americans, whose culture and cosmology is based upon this reality.

In recent years, the environmental movement has also made us aware of how connected we all are to every part of the worldwide ecosystem. When we eat a meal we selectively incorporate our environment into our body. The physicist David Bohm wrote:

> As the plant is formed, maintained and dissolved by the exchange of matter and energy with its environment, at which point can we say that there is a sharp distinction between what is alive and what is not? Clearly, a molecule of carbon dioxide that crosses a cell boundary into a leaf does not suddenly "come alive" nor does a molecule of oxygen suddenly "die" when it is released to the atmosphere. Rather, life itself has to be regarded as belonging in some sense to a totality, including plant and environment.[13]

For many years before the revelations of quantum physics, people believed the universe was like a machine—that it was predictable in a mechanical way and that it was made up of separate objects. At one level this view serves us. The trajectory of a ball or a rocket can be calculated from this perspective, for instance. However, in the early twentieth century this mechanistic view came into question, and with the advancement of quantum physics a whole new way of perceiving the universe emerged.

Quantum physics tells us that we are composed of something so small that it is vibration, emptiness, the unseen, and that in an interconnected way, change in one place affects change in another. What we perceive as matter is primarily empty space, and life arises out of something unseen—a kind of vibration that can only be known by perceiving its effects. This is the quantum level—the heart of matter.

We can take into account the unseen quantum reality of the physical world and the unseen personal reality of each person. From this perspective, there are, in the most basic way of speaking, two unseen realities. They seem to come together in what we call mind.

Systems (chaos) theory evolved along with quantum physics. This science tells us that at the quantum level unseen systems organize everything. These systems create order out of chaos in increasing complexity and diversity. From this perspective they work like mind and we interact with them. Some people simply say, "It is God working in a mysterious way."

Chapter XXVII

The Strangest Paradox

Since freedom powers our individuality, allowing us to define ourselves and to create meaning, our freedom to choose is godlike.

On our journey of exploration through the maze of senseless behaviors woven into our world, we've confronted some very strange paradoxes, but the strangest of all lies just ahead: that we are a part of All and apart from All, essentially both separate and *already* connected. Let's take a look, because somehow our freedom from oppression hinges on our understanding this.

Paradoxically, we can most fully experience our separateness when we fully experience our inner-connectedness, that is, our connection to self, as well as our interconnectedness, that is, our connection to all. We have seen that people who do not know their inner-connectedness, at least intellectually, behave as if they *were* someone else; *I am you—so close, that I know what you're thinking, intending, etc.*

Religion and science not only shed light on unseen realities and our interconnectedness, but also lead us to the understanding that we are also, paradoxically, separate. Religions, for example, not only tell us that we are interconnected, but also they tell us that we are responsible for our individual selves. Science not only tells us that we are all interconnected—the *act* of observing affects the observed—but also that there *is* an observer who is the *separate* actor.

Another way to understand the paradox of being both separate and connected at once is to know that you are in one sense apart from nature (observing it) and in another sense you are a part of nature (formed from it).

Even the personal experience of unity demonstrates our separateness and simultaneous connectedness. When people experience themselves as being at one with all, they also experience themselves as *separate* and apart-from-all. They are autonomous and fully functional in their everyday lives. They can talk about their experiences and remember them. They are not dissolved in oneness. If they were dissolved into oneness there would be no separate self to have the experience and to remember it.

That we are both connected and separate is a fact of extra-ordinary significance, because from all evidence this knowledge proves to be highly effective in dissolving the need and inclination to connect backwards.

For instance, a woman with whom I consulted connected to her daughter in a backwards way: "You don't want to do that." "You don't know what you're talking about." "That's not what you think." "You'll never amount to anything." For more than thirty years the daughter had tried to get her mother to see her and to hear her. But the mother, whom I shall call Vie, had only related to her "pretend daughter." Vie "knew" what her daughter meant, wanted, should do, was trying to do, what would happen to her in the future, and so forth.

After I talked with Vie, and she attended one of my workshops, she could see that she had acted irrationally toward her daughter. Once Vie understood that no one could know the things that she was pretending to know about her daughter, that they were spellbinding illusions, that her daughter was *separate*, and, most important, that they had even more than a genetic connection, that they were *connected* in spirit, she woke up to what she had been doing.

She was surprised when she realized that she'd been attempting to control her daughter. She'd been utterly unaware of the impact of her comments.

Vie let go of her pretend daughter. She opened to her inner-connectedness despite the pain she found within. Facing her inner experience, she gradually built a strong connection to herself. No longer beside herself, Vie was able to stand separate from her daughter. She could see her and hear her "as if she were a separate person." Vie made such progress that she was even able to ask her daughter to let her know if she forgot herself and momentarily connected backwards. Her daughter watched for the spell and showed it to her mother when it came around. Finally, Vie overcame it.

We know our separateness in many ways. For instance, we have our own personal realities within our psychic boundaries; we have the freedom to choose; we are self-defining; and we have individual identities. Let's look briefly at our separateness within our connectedness.

Like a cell, each of us is separate and at the same time "part" of a greater totality. In fact, our psychic boundary not only distinguishes us as separate but also enables others to relate to us. When two people communicate with each other, if either person's identity is *not* distinct and separate, there is no "other" with whom to relate.

In relationships, if people don't see their partners as separate they cannot love. For example, when a batterer says, "I loved her too much!" he is not speaking of "her" but of Teddy. In this situation, when a real person displaces Teddy, the real person is battered.

The spell, including the Teddy Illusion, gives us a way to know about and talk about Control Connections and what it's like to be the object of someone's illusions. It allows us to understand why people behave irrationally, why they attempt to control others, why they cannot see and respect the other's separateness, and consequently, why they move against the compelling force no matter what their intentions.

The exploration of our paradoxical connectedness and simultaneous separateness leads us to a great treasure. This treasure is something that helps explain this paradox and something that oppressive and controlling behaviors directly oppose. The treasure is freedom.

Freedom, like consciousness, arises out of the universal and runs through us like God coming into the world. Through freedom we are all connected. In this respect, freedom links our separateness and our connectedness. It both belongs to each of us and it belongs to all. It is individualized in each of us when we make choices. When we exercise our freedom, tapping into the universal, we affirm and experience our separateness.

Our ability to choose is our most basic freedom. When we define ourselves we choose. When we give meaning to our experience we also choose. The more aware we are of ourselves and our day-to-day experience, the more we are able to exercise freedom's power—the power of choice. Freedom depends upon clarity. We cannot exercise our freedom if we are confused. And, of course, being defined backwards leaves people confused. Backwards connections arise out of the Controller's confusion, and oppressive and controlling behaviors create confusion. When others define us, our freedom is assaulted because our awareness is assaulted.

Awareness and freedom are intrinsically linked. Without freedom awareness fades. Without awareness freedom fades. If our freedom of choice is lost, life itself loses meaning. Despair fills the void of lost meaning.

When Jack, whom we met at the beginning of our journey, was defined backwards, i.e., from the outside in, he became confused. His freedom to define himself and to make meaning of his experience was taken from him. "I guess I'm not hurt."

In a profound way, the very behavior that assaults freedom both denies freedom's universality (connectedness) and its unique expression (separateness).

In the next chapter we will enter spellbreaking territory. Everything we've found thus far will serve us. We've seen how and why people create Control Connections as well as what compels them. Now it is clear that breaking the spell not only preserves our freedom, but freedom itself. Becoming a Spellbreaker is a matter of conscience.

Chapter XXVIII

Breaking the Spell

The spell can be broken only by remembering how one has fallen under its influence, the words and incantations used.

In a certain sense the spell wants to be broken, because it is a collection of illusions that oppose the compelling force.

I invite you to imagine the force as a fast-moving but relatively shallow stream. The more people move against the stream, the more turbulent it becomes. If a hundred people were all wading upstream together, we would see a dam forming, about to break, to inundate the people, rather like a war that touches everyone.

So it is with us. If people connect in backwards ways, they move against the compelling force, in this case, the force of human consciousness seeking to know and to experience its own connectedness.

We have seen that people-problems (as distinguished from such problems as droughts, disease, and other natural disasters) range in their effects from mental anguish and emotional pain to some form of war in homes, streets, and countries. Verbal abuse, battering, stalking, harassment, hate crimes, gang violence, tyranny, terrorism, and territorial invasion are attempts by the Spellbound to control others.

The distress and discord that permeate the lives of millions are clear messages meant to tell us something. Just as a searing physical pain says something is wrong, so, too, does the psychic pain that floats through the world. Whatever form it takes, it is a sign that people have forgotten what is real and what is not, what is pretend and what is not, who they are and who they are not.

Can we find ways to remember, to fill the void, the abyss that beckons the disconnected and despairing to act against others and sometimes even against themselves? Is there anything to be done to break the spell, now, when it's been here for so long?

Does it take a great heroic act to make a life-affirming difference? Would a Witness have to lead an army, become a missionary, or join a rebel's ranks to bring awareness to a troubled world, to be spellbreaking? I think not.

Early in our journey through the maze of senseless behaviors woven into our world we explored the importance of context. We found that if we know the context in which something occurs we can make sense of it. People who have forgotten themselves, who have forgotten their connectedness and how they became disconnected, who have forgotten how they have forged counterfeit connections, and who, all along, thought the other *was* Teddy, are realizing that the primary context within which to perceive others is that they are *others*, i.e., separate people.

The other is a separate person with a separate reality who shares a common humanity. People are hearing the other. They are remembering their separateness and they are courageously remembering themselves.

> *Today I realized she is not the problem, only a reminder of the real issue.*
>
> —*S.N.*

If they are willing, the Spellbound can awake from their dream world by seeing the spell for what it is, and by remembering how they fell under it. By courageously facing their separateness and trusting in their true connectedness, they can find the strength to stand on their own two feet, apart from the other. If they accept the reality of their interconnectedness as well as the reality of their separateness, they can, with this two-fold awareness, begin to render possible what had before seemed impossible. They can break the spell's influence over them. And they can bring awareness to others.

Courage enables the Spellbound to persevere, to build inner connections to themselves and empathetic connections to others, to move toward truth no matter how frightened they are.

A Spellbreaker's goal is to be ever more alert to spellbinding behavior, to wake up Spellbound people, to call attention to the problem, and to enlighten those who have connected backwards to another person or group so that Spellbound people can move from unconscious controlling tactics to conscious and mutually beneficial behaviors.

We'll explore spell-breaking territory to find some ways to break the spell, keeping in mind that in some places and in some circumstances it can't be broken. Rather, like a toxic mist, it will eventually dissipate in the light of collective awareness.

Even now there is a new awareness that living disconnected is getting more difficult. It is simply not worth it, and connecting backwards is not any better. More and more Witnesses are responding to oppressive behaviors in ways that serve as a wake-up call to the Spellbound.

Controllers are learning that they get the opposite of what they want when they are under the influence of the spell. When they see the spell for what it is, they want to get out from under it. They don't want to live out their lives ensnared in an illusion.

Controllers are noticing that:

- When they diminish someone while believing that they have not shown feelings of inferiority, but rather their own superiority, they have it backwards.
- When they object to another person's ideas and opinions while believing that they have not shown ignorance, but rather intelligence, they have it backwards.
- When they define someone while believing that they have not pushed them away, but rather are closer than ever, they have it backwards.
- When they give orders while believing that they have not shown their fear of separateness, but rather their fear-lessness, they have it backwards.

And, Witnesses are noticing that when people are beside themselves or have learned who to be against, they do not act rationally. They play "Let's Pretend."

Daily, more and more Witnesses are noticing the nonsense they hear. When someone defines them, they no longer explain themselves, nor do they ask themselves, "What am I doing wrong?" Instead they ask "Who's making something up, playing let's pretend?"

Let's look at some defining statements to see just how irrational they are.

- You think you're smarter than anyone. You think I can just whip this out. You don't realize how hard I work. You just think I'm a jerk.

  No one knows what you think or what you realize.

- You don't have to write this down, just remember it.

  You may need to write it down to remember it.

- You're asking for trouble.

  You're asking for help or something else.

- You're attacking me.

  You've just said what bothers you.

- You wish I'd be hit by a truck!

This last nonsensical comment was reported by a Witness just yesterday. It's real, as they all are. And, of course, no one knows what you wish.

Although it's obvious that the defining statements above

are "silly talk," Witnesses have spent countless hours arguing against just such comments, trying to get Pretenders to stop pretending, to stop making up what they think, want, mean, wish, etc. But not for long. More and more Witnesses are realizing that arguing and explaining are wasted efforts expended on people who can't hear authentic people. Comments that define them are either confabulations designed to explain fear and anger over signs of separateness, or attempts to diminish authentic person to make room for a Pretend Person.

A spell-breaking response to nonsense, in one word, is, "What?" When I first used it, I didn't think it was going to be particularly effective. Surely, I thought, I could have come up with something really clever. But now as time has passed, I realize that this response is very effective. I didn't fall into the trap of trying to explain myself, and "What?" is useful for many reasons.

Nonsense can't be understood. By saying "What?" Spellbreakers don't give Controllers the impression that their let's-pretend world is real. In fact, they don't even want to try once they clearly understand that irrational behavior is a sign of the spell.

When a Spellbreaker responds to nonsense by saying, "What?" the Controller usually says something else just as nonsensical. To be effective the Witness again says, "What?" and so on.

If you hear someone telling you what you should do, are, have been, etc., and you say "What?" several good things happen.

1. You "can't hear" nonsense so you don't take it in, wonder about it, try to figure it out, or explain why it's not so.
2. By saying "What?" you can't be accused of interrupting. After all, you're only asking for clarity and it is

the responsibility of the person speaking to speak sensibly and to try again if they haven't made sense.

3. The person who just spoke to you has an opportunity to think, "Now what did I just say?" and possibly to retract the senseless talk and turn it into mindful talk.

4. The person who has attempted to define you finds it impossible to do so.

5. Each time you say "What?" the person who defines you has another opportunity to remember what was said, and to wake up from the spell.

If you have asked a question and are not hearing an appropriate response, simply repeat your question.

When a couple is dedicated to breaking the spell, I invite them to bond together against it. I often suggest that they choose a regular time for nurturing conversation—a date, a half hour, two or three times a week. Some describe it as a sacred time.

Following are some guidelines:

1. If either person hears the other defining them, they say, "What?" This gives the person who just spoke a chance to hear himself or herself and to respond appropriately, to say, for instance, "I don't know why I said that." Or, "That didn't come out right, I meant to say . . ."

2. Both people enter into the communication with the intention of hearing, responding, and reaching out to the other in a kind and understanding way.

3. Serious Spellbreakers keep their own tape recorders turned on, and on the table, so they can play back what they said, just in case they forget themselves.

Breaking a Control Connection may seem a simple task, but it is very hard for chronic Controllers to stand on their own two feet. The freedom of being separate, of remembering themselves, and of developing their inner-connectedness, of letting "Teddy" go, feels like death to the Controller. *If I am separate where will I be? What will I be connected to?* On the other hand, it is not easy for Witnesses to just say, "What?"

Unless Witnesses fully understand Control Connections and the compelling force behind them, they usually want to explain themselves: "That's not what I thought," or "That's not what I meant," etc. They want so very much to be heard and seen by the very person, who at the moment, cannot hear them or see them.

> *One of the questions I have struggled with is why was I so blind and unable to hear her as she expressed herself?*
>
> *—V.C., Arizona*

Some actions *against* people are known to be so evil that they are taboo, and some actions *for* people are treated as taboos because they jeopardize Control Connections and bonds against others.

For instance, some Witnesses who are under the influence of people who are under the influence of the spell fear that if they speak up, take care of themselves, and pursue their own interests, they will be shunned. And in some places they are. Some believe that if they object to other people's definitions of them they will be attacked, and in some places they are. To some, breaking the spell is like breaking a taboo.

If you doubt yourself, ask if the thoughts that are passing through your mind originated with something you heard about yourself or the way you were treated. If you feel frozen, unable to act or to come to a decision, possibly your choices, acts, and ideas have been countered, disparaged, or trivialized.

Rather than jeopardize their individuality, some people seek political asylum or leave abusive environments. They seek environments where others do not assault their physical and/or psychic boundaries. Nevertheless, some Witnesses feel that they are unable to leave a hurtful relationship even when it is within their own and their children's best interests to do so. They feel that they are breaking a taboo to strike out on their own. Moving against the spell fills them with dread—the feeling that they are doomed.

Women, especially, may have been told that they should be able to make their relationships work, no matter what, or that self-reliance is unfeminine. Men in particular may have been told they should be in charge of other adults, should never give up or admit to a mistake or to being hurt. These teachings not only erroneously define women and men, but also deepen the spell.

In some cultures, if you break a Control Connection, you are shunned, alienated from the society that originally created the taboo, the one you have known, the one from which you seek acceptance. Even their God, they say, will turn against you. But making up what God will do is just another way of establishing a backwards connection. Even keeping a relationship but at a distance may be forbidden in very oppressive families.

A brilliant young woman immersed in her family culture was told by her parents that she couldn't go to an excellent university even though she was accepted, even though all her expenses would be paid. Why? Because her family defined her as a household companion. They simply liked having her around.

She broke her family's Control Connection by leaving and accepting the opportunity her merits afforded her. Although her family called their attempt to control her a tradition, she had the courage to break the spell. By choosing to live her own life, she transformed from a Witness into a Spellbreaker.

Catching the spell descending can sometimes stop its progress. Jean had been dating Jay for almost a year when she called to discuss strategies that she hoped would wake him up. Jay was a fun guy, well respected in his profession, and well thought of by his colleagues. But he had started saying "weird stuff" to Jean. Jean wanted to be a Spellbreaker. She hoped to wake him up to his "weirdness."

"What does he say?" I asked.

"For instance," she said, "we went out to a nice restaurant for dinner and I ordered my favorites, then he said, 'You have terrible taste.' I was flabbergasted. I didn't know what to say. How can I deal with this kind of behavior? He's saying things like this quite a lot."

(I thought Jean would probably have plenty of opportunities to say, "What?" And I wondered if Jay could have met Joe, whom we met earlier in the pizza/linguini incident.) In order to prepare Jay for a change in Jean's behavior and to give him an opportunity to wake up, I proposed a plan to Jean.

What do you think about this? When next you see him, do you think you could tell him something like this? "For some strange reason, in a way that's hard to describe, I occasionally hear you say something that sounds as if you were pretending to be me. Have you ever felt like you were me?"

If you choose to follow up on this idea and actually say this to him, it's likely he'll say your question sounds absurd and whatever are you talking about? That would be the time to say, "It's hard for me to describe, but in the future if I do get this impression, I'll just say, 'What?' 'til I see what's happening."

It's likely he won't mind. May not even hear what you're telling him.

Jean tried this approach. Gradually, Jay noticed what he was doing.

Mary and Mick got along for a while. Then after they married, Mick began to fall under the spell. For instance, Mary asked Mick how he felt about a problem she'd had at work. In an angry voice, Mick said, "I told you what I thought when I called. You just weren't listening."

Her message machine gave her proof that she wasn't crazy. They hadn't talked since she'd left the message telling him of the problem. And Mary knew he hadn't even mentioned the situation in his phone messages to her. (Of course dream woman *would* know what he thought.)

She didn't doubt herself, but still she didn't know how to deal with this kind of nonsense. She felt like saying, "You're a liar," or "You're hallucinating," but she knew name-calling and accusing weren't the right responses.

She thought about telling him he hadn't left any comment like that. But he had a way of diverting her and of arguing against her so relentlessly that there was no chance of reconciliation. More and more often, when this kind of thing happened she buried her feelings, swallowed her pain, and said nothing.

As we talked she began to see that the possible core of the problem was that Mick had already taken up residence within her via his pretend woman. She saw that if this were the case, his Teddy would never have asked him what he thought, Teddy would know! (No wonder he was angry. Mary was showing signs of separateness.)

Mary also realized that when Mick told her, "You weren't listening," just as if he lived within her, he was speaking nonsense. Mary decided not to take in the nonsense. It was gobbledygook. She couldn't hear it. Consequently, "What?" was her response of choice. Mick began to wake up from the spell that had just begun to overtake him. He got help, and he got better.

Just as I wrote the word "better," I got a call from the East Coast that reminded me I'd better mention when NOT to say "What?" Sometimes saying "What?" is not the best choice.

Married for twenty-seven years, Mrs. A. said she'd read my books on verbal abuse and that her husband had gotten pretty aggressive defining her, calling her a lot of names. Things had gotten worse very gradually, but recently they were really awful. And with children still at home she'd tried to cope.

"What kind of names?"

"Bad ones."

I had a very strong feeling that she wasn't talking about the average Spellbound Controller.

"Ever been hit?" I asked.

"Yes, but I told the doctor the injuries were from something else, but I can change that." she said.

"That would be a very positive step. Any income?"

"Yes, but he hasn't paid taxes in twenty-five years."

"Any weapons?"

"He bought an assault weapon and said he'd kill me if I left."

"Whoa! You haven't got a husband. You've got a criminal." Don't say "What?"

- To a person who has threatened your life
- To a person who lies for no apparent reason
- To a person in a rage
- To a person who displays a weapon in a threatening way around you
- To a person who is following you
- To a stranger

I told my caller her best contacts were (1) a shelter (most help both men and women), (2) an attorney, and (3) the police (in any crisis).

Another caller said that in couple's counseling she told the counselor of a terrifying event, a demonstration of rage "in her face." The counselor brushed it off. Then when she brought it up again saying she was still afraid, the counselor said, "He's never going to do it again, so just drop it."

This counselor seemed to be deeply immersed in the spell, pretending to know the husband's future, forever and ever, giving orders and failing to acknowledge my caller's fear. Sometimes there is a fairy tale quality to the spell. People so influenced make up a fairy tale, a "happy ever after" ending.

While the Spellbound counselor had no clue, Spellbreakers, including many counselors, can spot the spell pretty fast, even if they don't have a name for it. They feel uncomfortable or angry when they observe or experience oppressive behaviors. They feel an aura of unreality when someone says one thing and then later pretends to have said something quite different. They have a sinking feeling or feel apprehensive. Their own inner "radar" spots the spell and even rings a bell, warning them that a Spellbound person is close.

When Spellbreakers speak up to break Control Connections, they do it with courage. In some workplaces they have been threatened, demoted, harassed, or fired for being Spellbreakers.

Spell-breaking Strategies
- Recognize the reality of your inner truth.
- Be aware of boundary invasions, yours or anyone else's.
- Do not respond to nonsense as if it made sense.
- Build your life on truth.
- Protect your children.
- Speak up to break the spell.
- If someone defines you, say either

"What?"

"What did you say?"

"I heard that."

"Nonsense."

or

"What are you doing?"

If you are defined, harassed, or put down in any way at work, write it down. As you take out your notebook and pen, ask spell-breaking questions: "What did you say? Do you have the time? How do you spell your last name?"

If the spell can't be broken, if you are with a Spellbound person who will not change, your spiritual, if not your physical survival may depend upon your escaping.

Spellbound people can show up on radio and television, defining others and haranguing against people who aren't just like them. Spellbreakers change the station or the channel. If enough people do so, the spellbound person has no audience and the spell becomes weaker instead of stronger.

Growing Up: Spellbound or Spellbreaker?

It is spell-breaking to tell a child who is defined by another child or by an adult, "What he or she said to you just now is not okay. He or she is pretending."

Parents, teachers, and all who influence others can be Spellbreakers by teaching the difference between what is pretend and what is not. When they see someone discriminated against, bullied, or harassed, they can talk about the courage and heroism it takes to bond together *for* rather than *against* the other.

Support of our children includes teaching them that encountering boundaries is encountering life. For instance, there are limits to what we can know about another person:

"Saying that your friend is stupid is only pretending to know how intelligent she is. Do you mean to say that you are angry about something?"

In times past some people thought that, like the miller's daughter in the earlier story, women must struggle through years of trials to gain their strength. They thought that this was fundamentally necessary for psychological growth, as though women were born with an unfortunate psychological deficit.

However, the feminine struggle to overcome oppression is, like that of all people who are oppressed, an attempt to break the spell. In all times and in all places where men and women have been oppressed, they have had to escape if they could not break the spell. They have had to stop the oppressor's relentless effort to control them.

People who encounter Controllers seek solutions, and they struggle for equal treatment, from protesting in marches and sit-ins to declaring that an accusation or harassment is intolerable. They fight oppression, from taking up arms against invaders to taking up humanitarian causes.

Attempts to control others betray millions, dismantling entire countries and destroying the lives of the innocent. For these reasons, people are stepping forward dedicated to breaking the spell, hopeful of bringing us closer to a more real, more honest way of interacting—a more real and more honest world, certainly a less frightening and shocking one.

Although there are many ways to see and solve a problem, I believe that seeing this problem as a problem of connection will help immunize us from it, even put it down if it has gotten the upper hand. We will see how absurd it is, and we won't be inclined to believe or to accept anyone's definition of us, or of anyone else, even if they're in a prestigious or authoritative position. In fact, I believe that if enough of us see the problem for what it is, it will begin to disappear like a shadow brought to light.

Many people who chronically indulge in oppressive behaviors have said that they felt compelled to contact me. They want to stop. They want to change, although they often have little or no idea what that change involves, nor do they know why they find it difficult to stop trying to control others when they really do want to stop. Nonetheless, they trust that change is possible. This good news suggests that even though a Control Connection may seem, at times, to be better than no connection at all, Controllers are wakening to the knowledge that there is a better way to connect—a less stressful and extraordinarily more satisfying one.

They have found the courage to change because they want to leave the world a better place for generations after them, and because they have come to the realization that as long as they avoid this challenge, life will become ever more difficult.

> *I want this to end in my generation, and I want that feeling I had one time when I was different—when I wasn't controlling.*
>
> *—L.N., Washington*

Chapter XXIX

Clarity

If it weren't for people like you wanting to change, there would be no change in the world.

I f, by chance, you find that you have been Spellbound, pretending that you knew someone else's personal reality, you can cast off the spell if you desire. Although it is powerful, a spell is *only* an influence. Just knowing about it can lessen its power over you.

On the other hand, if you have heard defining statements and thought they came from *reason*, or that someone was *there* to whom you could explain yourself, knowledge of the spell and how people can be beside themselves makes it clear that this is not the case. Defining statements are illusory indeed. And when people are beside themselves, they are not "there" to hear the truth.

Even though many Controllers want to change, some are under so many influences, cultural prescriptions, backwards perceptions, lost selves, disconnections, and so forth, that they are inclined to stay Spellbound as long as they live, clinging to whatever identity they've constructed and to whatever anchor seems to work.

They don't have to relate to a real person to feel close, because they are close to their illusory person or group. In fact, some Controllers definitely choose not to change. One posted a sign in his office, "I will not change." I saw it as a mantra relentlessly reminding him of his insistence on remaining Spellbound and his determination to avoid awareness.

Although most people are conscious of their behavior, the more deeply Spellbound are unconscious of its impact. At the extreme, some individuals become so disconnected from themselves that they are like two different people, unconscious even of what they've said and done. But many Controllers want desperately to break the spell's hold over them, especially when they see that some of the ways they have been trained to behave and some of the ways they have learned to cope have backwards results that both harm others and get themselves the opposite of what they want.

*How long would it take to change? What can I do
to change? Do you know of people who have successfully changed? How can I ensure the change?*
—M.L., New York

To break the spell's hold, Controllers must face their fear
of separateness and the loss of their "perfect" identity, the one
they built backwards, from the outside in. Can they see what
they are doing and address their fears in such a way that they
are not compelled to act against others? How can they gain the
knowledge lost and the experience forsaken that would have
allowed them to know themselves? Let's look at how the spell
disintegrates in the light of awareness.

I am a Controller. I have been living Spellbound.
*Regardless of the reasons and insights into my past
and how I was treated and abused, my behavior and
wounding of another is wrong. I was blind to all my
abusive ways and the tactics I used.*
*While I was aware of my anger just under the sur-
face and I was aware of the fact that sometimes I
intentionally hurt my partner, I thought, "That wasn't
that bad, others have it worse." I dehumanized and
devalued the most valuable and precious person I
know. I didn't hear her or see her. I am taking steps to
be accountable to others and whatever else it takes to
get healing.*
*I am realizing that this may just take years. That's
okay. I plan on changing for the rest of my earthly life.*
—G.H., Georgia

When people wake up to the impact of their behavior and
when they find out what they're missing, they usually want to be

connected within themselves, rather than within someone else. They want to experience the reality of their connectedness. They want to feel like they felt as very young children when they were still connected, when they were so small they could not put their experience into words.

I've met a number of people who are realizing that we are all interconnected in a most mysterious way and that we are also all separate. They are breaking the spell's hold over them.

> *I am thankful for the opportunity to see the spell unraveled and the knowledge disseminated.*
> —*A.N., Colorado*

As we've seen, people who have established Control Connections usually respond to signs of separateness with anger. Managing anger is important, but knowing why one is angry is essential!

A man of high intelligence, articulate and sophisticated, realized *why* he was angry during a phone consultation. The moment in which he became angry was particularly revealing. During our discussion, he fought the pervasive and ancient spell and came to grips with its reality in his own life. He was striving to be aware. He was being careful not to fall under the spell. He was working hard to be a Spellbreaker.

He and his wife had been communicating openly. They had enjoyed supportive conversations. Then one day he was gripped by the spell in a spell-binding moment. Here's how he described his experience to me and how he woke from his illusions.

> *"I saw her giving a presentation to our sales staff and I was filled with rage. I didn't say a word, but anger seethed from me. She saw my narrowed eyes, my clenched fists, my hostility.*

"My rationale: She wasn't talking and explaining things the way I would.

"Later she called me on it. She was angry and called me an ass, and I got mad that she did that. I'd only made one slip. I thought I was doing so well. I hadn't yelled at her or hit her. And she says she'd just started to trust me, and now she doesn't, and I'm back to square one and I think she should apologize for calling me an ass."

"I'd like to go back to the core problem," I told him. "Could you do that with me by imagining something for me?"

He agreed.

"I'd like you to look at your hand. Now imagine that as you're looking at your hand, you intend to pick up your coffee cup, but your hand is reaching for some papers lying nearby. Can you see it? Again, look at your coffee cup, watching it, and out of the corner of your eye do you see your hand going for the papers?"

I asked him to do this several times. Then I asked, "What do you feel?"

"I want to rage at my hand in fury. How dare it. I want to yell loud. I want to MAKE it do what I want. I want to control it.

"Oh, this is exactly what I felt when she was talking. Seeing everyone sitting there approving of her talk only made it worse. She seemed so . . ."

"Separate?" I asked.

"Yes. I felt just so powerless."

"Possibly," I said, "when you saw her as a hand, as Teddy, as who you wanted her to be, through your eyes she did not feel like a person, but annihilated, and that's why she was angry and called you an ass."

Later, he shared his thoughts, holding the hope that his "personal struggle will benefit others." In doing so, he forges a spell-breaking path.

"I can understand that she is still angry and hurt. I had no idea that this process would take so long.

"No wonder I thought I had a wonderful relationship but my real wife wasn't in the picture. I couldn't hear her pain.

"The metaphor of the hand was perfect for me. That is exactly what happens. As horrible and violent as the word 'annihilation' is, I have to say that it is accurate. The sheer force of the word helps me to realize the importance of staying awake, aware. I don't want to be under the spell.

"The spell is so important for me to understand.

"I thought more about it, was able to remember the ways that this was how I was treated and related to as a child. I had no separateness, no identity. I was the hand at times, being the object of the anger at not 'moving' in the proper way. So along with the deprivation of affection there was the annihilation of my individuality."

A great many people don't define anyone, nor do they replace an empathetic connection with a backwards, outside-in connection. They live their lives meeting difficult challenges, even feeling afraid and alone at times. Still, they don't make up people or the world around them unless they momentarily forget themselves. But as we saw on our journey through the maze of senseless behaviors woven into our world, many people are beside themselves most of the time.

Since thousands of people have contacted me about the problem, I am certain that Control Connections abound. Historically, they've existed for a long, long time.

Illusions come to life in early childhood. When children find their world unbearable, when their basic needs are not met, they may create a Pretend Person or a pretend world. Being in control and connected to their pretend world, they feel secure.

> *I am sometimes very discouraged at how entangled this whole mess is. The pretend world I created still overlaps the new world that I am starting to live in. It is so hard to reorient myself. I really see, I was connected backwards to her.*
>
> *—M.V., Ontario*

Some people have not learned to know what their feelings mean. Some have been trained not to feel much. And some have been trained not to know that they have feelings.

> *"My wife has this talent," said a client.*
> *"What's that?"*
> *"Well, she has feelings," he said.*

Controllers feel the pain and anxiety of disconnection when giving up their Control Connections. The process is not easy—even to those who know that an empathic connection is a source of joy.

Typically, as they wake from the spell, they become active in giving up their backwards connections. Some even monitor their own thoughts, stopping irrational thinking that pretends to know the other.

Following are some comments from people who are getting out from under the spell:

- "Every day is a new discovery, some painful, some healing, all beneficial."

- "I am aware that I have a very hard time expressing what I really want and need."
- "I am glad to wake up from the dream and come alive to feelings and life. I am hopeful that I will be able to share this life with others. I do want to nourish and give life."
- "Because of your concern and passion to see people whole and relationships real, I am indebted to you and others who share this vision."
- "It's like rehabilitation from an injury. Things are slow-going, but I think that I see progress. Some progress *is* progress. I see change."
- "I realize I've been treating my children like dream children."
- "We can now talk about anything and I can hear some of her questions, feel pain, and admit to the abuse and control. I have felt a closeness that is growing slooooooowly. I am so careful to not fall under the spell. In fact, I told her that I am afraid of doing that and need her to tell me when it happens. I told her how much I appreciate the fact that she has been doing double duty—dealing with her emotions and monitoring my behaviors."
- "Forced to confront my fears, I am surviving and I'm learning to be secure in myself. In effect, my destructive behavior has led to its own destruction."

The knowledge of separateness is a wand that breaks the spell. Those who are caught in its grip can choose to take up the wand, but all success depends upon courage.

It takes tremendous courage to stand on one's own two feet. Separate. It takes time to work through all the pain held at bay by Control Connections.

I was wrong. I have been so selfish. I wish my growth was faster but mighty oaks take time to mature. I want to be that oak.

—L.V., San Francisco

Even after knowing why they could not be seen and heard, Witnesses also find that recovery takes a long time.

Now, five years later, I'm just starting to feel normal. I was defined for years.

—S.R., Texas

Living beside themselves, disconnected from their inner depths, the Spellbound have experienced only the surface of life. Their shallow perception prevented them from recognizing the rich depth of real people. Understanding and appreciating life's diversity goes a long way toward ending prejudice and discrimination against others.

Most of us admire, even stand in awe of the miracle of human individuality. Likewise we admire, even stand in awe of nature's individuation: a sunset, an orchid, a newborn fawn, a snow-capped mountain, a baby, a hummingbird's nest. But some Spellbound people are just beginning to see how awesome difference is.

Waking from the spell, many former Controllers, rather than fearing difference and separateness, have begun to honor individuality, the magic of creation—an ever changing kaleidoscope of form, color, pattern, movement, and personal perspective.

I realize that we can both look at the same thing but that we each have our own view. And I realize I can appreciate these differing perspectives. Agreement and appreciation are not about being of one mind but about sharing and community

I am getting better at being separate as well as seeing my wife as separate. I am constantly thinking of how to be the best friend my wife needs. This is a great help.

—J.D., Nebraska

Even as no two fingerprints are the same, no two people are the same. Since nature flows into distinction, and so is constantly expanding in diversity, honoring different people, different views, and separateness itself is a way of respecting life and breaking the spell.

When Controllers let go of Pretend Person and their grip within the other, they no longer have the protection of a backwards connection. Giving up the anchor of Pretend Person planted in someone is frightening to Controllers. But feeling their pain and fear brings them back to themselves. The fruits of such an endeavor are the gifts of empathy and, ultimately, true inner connection. The inclination to connect backwards diminishes as awareness of inner connection increases.

As former Controllers grieve their losses and attend to their feelings, they re-establish their inner connection, and their empathy reconnects them to others.

I am glad of the growth and maturation that I am going through. I have come to a place from which I can no longer return. I am able to slow down my thinking and identify feelings.

—B.J., Iowa

Instead of acting to keep Pretend Person "alive" by means of fear, intimidation, and dominance, former Controllers find that they can accept and give love freely. Their strength flows from spirit full enough to nurture another, alive enough to act toward good, clear enough to understand, faithful enough to wait and see, fearless enough to reveal the truth, free enough to choose to learn, courageous enough to stand alone, connected enough to love the other.

Understanding how I have defined others has brought great freedom to my life.
　　　　　　　　　　　　　　　　—S.G., North Carolina

Chapter XXX

Aligned with the Compelling Force

So long have they been unseen and unheard, their wonder fills the space where they exist, the wonder that they exist at all.

A wareness of our true connectedness evokes respect like galaxies evoke wonder. Inner connection deepens our vision, enabling us to see beneath the surface, beyond appearances. Inner connection aligns us with the compelling force.

When we are open to our experience, that is, to our feelings, intuitions, and sensations, we are better able to spot the spell even at a distance. In this way we are aligned with the compelling force that has always advanced toward increasing awareness of our connectedness, hence toward casting off the spell.

Our longing for awareness is a holy quest that, in and of itself, lends meaning and purpose to life. We yearn for meaning the way a plant yearns for the sun. If it were not where the plant sought it, the plant would lose life. If the meaning we seek is not where we have grown to expect it, we too can lose life. Meaning renders satisfaction possible and makes our trials bearable. The loss of meaning threatens survival.

Throughout the world the seeds of chaos have been fostered in ignorance and grown in cultures unconscious of themselves. Control Connections are such seeds. They oppose both nature and the course of human evolution. Paradoxically, however, the havoc they wreak forces us to evolve out of unknowing into knowing.

Our journey of exploration through the maze of senseless behaviors woven into our world has been a quest for knowledge. We have sought to make sense of senseless behaviors, to find out what compels them and how to deal with them.

We have discovered the spell and learned how it was cast. We have heard the words and incantations used. We have learned that the need for connection is inherent in consciousness because consciousness *is* universal connection.

We have seen that some people, in their desire to experience their connectedness, have established sad substitutes for real connection simply because they have lost inner awareness.

They have built a door of misconceptions and locked themselves in. Over thousands of years they have struggled to open it, becoming ever more angry, ever more oppressive. But some have found the key that opens this door.

> *What helped me more than anything was the knowledge of disconnection and the realization that I was already connected.*
> —*R.T., Massachusetts*

When we are aligned with the compelling force, we are compelled to express and honor individuality. At the same time, our reverence for individuality further aligns us with the force. The outcome of such alliance is both rejuvenating and empowering.

People who are aligned with the compelling force feel real. They experience their true connectedness. They bond together for, rather than against, others. They stand by those who are diminished, defined, and attacked. They seek purpose and meaning while facing their fears with courage. They trust in the goodness of the universe, knowing that even subtle attempts to control others are signs of the spell. They are naturally self-defining.

Consciously choosing, they establish who and what they are, what they will and will not accept, what they like and don't like. In this way they articulate their reality and determine it with specific experience. This is self-creation. This is conscious choice-making.

Being aligned with the compelling force, they experience a deep security not otherwise possible. They know that the struggle to maintain backwards connections is never-ending and never satisfying. Such efforts sacrifice true autonomy on the altar of ignorance. Maintaining an illusory connection may well *be* the meaning and purpose of a life built backwards.

Alignment with the compelling force and awareness of inner connection connect us with others. The natural experience of empathy confirms our interconnectedness and generates our reverence for humanity, because empathy is an attribute of love and a function of human consciousness. But even when we experience empathy for others, their feelings will resonate differently within them than within us, because their personal reality is uniquely their own. No one can *fully* know the depth and breadth of another person's experience. Even so, empathy is possible. Words do not adequately describe this kind of awareness—this connection.

If we consider the fact that each one of us is *naturally* self-defining, it is easy to see that those who define us act against nature. Consequently, those who attempt to control others are facing an insurrection of consciousness both from within and from without. Ultimately the compelling force will not be turned back. It is constant and cannot be defeated. It is only the circumstances and events that change. Human consciousness will know its own connectedness because backwards connections are self-defeating.

Over and over again I have seen that those who cast off the spell thrive. It matters not whether they have been Spellbound or have been under the influence of the Spellbound. However, aligning with the compelling force does not mean that they encounter no difficulties. They usually do. But if they act on their own behalf with regard for others' separateness, they live in accordance with the dynamics of the universe. They align with the compelling force. And it supports them. As we seek to know and experience our own connectedness, our everyday encounters give us constant opportunities to align ourselves with the compelling force.

If Jack's parents had aligned with the force they would

have said, "Oh, you hurt your knee. Let's take care of it. Are you tired and hungry? Are you ready for lunch?" Isn't that what we do when we are hurt? Notice it. Take care of it. Take care of ourselves.

Aligned with the compelling force, we protect our separateness, demonstrating that we can neither accept nor take in nonsense. We recognize nonsense for what it is. When we stand up for freedom, truth, and mutuality, we are empowered. By honoring the distinct reality of the other, we honor the "intent" of the universe, and the universe supports us.

People who are aligned with the compelling force actually experience life in a different way than do those who move against it. For instance, they don't demand allegiance as do people who indulge in oppressive behaviors, because they have already earned the loyalty of those close to them.

While allegiance is demanded by the disconnected, loyalty makes no demand of anyone. It is like solid gold given freely, arising out of high regard and respect for a person, group, cause, or ideal. It is mindful and conscious.

People who are aligned with the compelling force also experience a personal relationship with God. Instead of attempting to appear "becoming to God," following one of dozens of prescriptions that tell us how to do this, they relinquish the struggle, knowing that God cannot be beguiled. They don't need to fight and kill to prove their prescription superior to others, as so many have done in "holy" wars both past and present. Instead, seeing a goal of wisdom and good in being godlike, they strive to behave as if they already were a part of all, even while simultaneously separate.

Witnesses and Spellbreakers are coming forward daily, ready to exercise their personal freedom to define themselves and to create meaningful lives. The power of collective awareness is bringing change to the world. Spellbound people are taking up their own journey, even out of places where the spell is deepest and darkest.

> *I have just started to climb my mountain. I pray that when I reach the top, all those I defined are there to embrace me. I have begun my ascent. They have already done all they can.*
>
> —*J.H., Canada*

Whether we are with it or against it, the compelling force is one we can count on. In one way or another it will always be with us, calling us to awareness, reminding us of what we have forgotten.

Afterword

I have shared the perspective presented in this book with people throughout the country. Yesterday, a woman called who had attended a workshop I had just given.

> *I want to tell you that I thought I knew what con-trol was about—that you wouldn't have much new to tell me—I'd read your books so many times. But, oh, you blew my mind. Now I finally know what was wrong. Do you know what that means to me? I can't begin to tell you.*
>
> *For years I couldn't understand why he'd look through me or walk away when I was talking, or put me down and say it was just teasing. I'd have spent my life wondering.*

When people call or write to me about their relationships, their anguish is deep, their disappointment and confusion intense. The following note is typical of many I receive. It was written by a person who was assaulted for years by subtle, oppressive acts. It was signed "anonymous."

> *Thousands of dollars were spent on the best counselors who, of course, blamed me for "our" problems. To this day, I do not know how or why I survive. I often thought of suicide and regularly wished to die. But I somehow continue. I see no point in spending money I don't have for counseling since the "best" served only to compound my disintegration.*
>
> *Please keep writing. I now know what happened to me. I just don't know why.*

The problem of control is so pervasive, the plea to understand so frequent, I have kept writing.

Bibliography

Bohm, David (1980). *Wholeness and the Implicate Order*. London: ARK paperbacks, imprint of Routledge & Kegan Paul plc.

de Becker, Gaven (1997). *The Gift of Fear*. Canada: Little Brown & Company.

Miller, Alice (Translated by Hildegarde and Hunter Hannum) (1983). *For Your Own Good: Hidden Cruelty in Child-Rearing and the Roots of Violence*. New York: Farrar, Straus, and Giroux.

Stark, E. and Flitcraft, A. (1988). "Women and Children at Risk: A Feminist Perspective on Child Abuse." *International Journal of Health Services*, 18(1), 97–118.

Survey

I invite you, the reader, to answer the following questionnaire so that we might know more about control tactics, the spell, and your experience of it. Your participation in this survey will be of value and is greatly appreciated. You do not in any way need to reveal your identity.

Please check the applicable response and add any additional notes you feel are appropriate. Return to:

Patricia Evans
Evans Interpersonal Communications Institute
P.O. Box 589
Alamo, CA 94507

Or for information, resources, and services:

Phone: 925-934-5972
Fax: 925-933-9636
E-mail: EVANSbooks@aol.com
www.PatriciaEvans.com
www.VerbalAbuse.com

Please include a self-addressed stamped envelope if you need a reply to your correspondence by mail.
I thank you in advance.

I am
☐ female   ☐ male

I am
☐ married   ☐ separated   ☐ married
☐ single   ☐ divorced

I am _____ years old.

I deal with a Spellbound person
☐ at work
☐ in my family
☐ in my relationship
☐ in school
☐ all of the above

I would describe myself as
- ☐ a Spellbreaker.
- ☐ under the spell.
- ☐ I have never been under the spell.
- ☐ I was under the spell but not anymore.

This book helped me to
- ☐ understand the spell
- ☐ recognize Spellbound people
- ☐ get out from under the spell
- ☐ use spell-breaking strategies
- ☐ other:_____

_____

_____

_____

_____

_____

What I need the most now is:

_____

_____

_____

_____

_____

_____

If you had an experience with the spell that you would like to share, please do so below.

When I was under the spell,
or
When I encountered a Spellbound person, I . . .

Endnotes

1. U.S. Department of Labor, Bureau of Labor Statistics, "Young women enroll in college in greater numbers than young men." Originally published June 30, 1999.

2. Welfare Reform Report, *Contra Costa Times,* by staff writer Meredith May, October 10, 1998.

3. *The Gift of Fear* by Gaven de Becker p. 174 (Little, Brown and Company, Canada, 1997).

4. "Research confirms that battering men often escalate violence to recapture battered women and children who have sought safety in separation. . . . As many as 75 percent of the visits to emergency rooms by battered women occur after separation" (Stark and Flitcraft, 1988). Permission to reprint granted by Barbara J. Hart, Legal Director, Pennsylvania Coalition Against Domestic Violence.

5. For more information on road rage see "Summary of Aggressive Driving Study" published by the American Automobile Association Foundation for Traffic Safety.

6. "The World: How to Commit the Perfect Dictatorship," *New York Times,* by Blaine Harden, Week in Review section, November 26, 2000.

7. "Word for Word," *New York Times,* by Joe Sharkey, Week in Review Desk, October 25, 1998.

8. "Cult Controversy in Berkeley, Heavens Gate Survivor Takes Message to UC Berkeley," *San Francisco Chronicle,* by staff writer Alex Barnun, August 22, 1997.

9. For more information about child labor, see *The Atlantic Monthly,* February 1996: "Child Labor in Pakistan," Volume 227, No. 2, pp. 27–92.

10. For an in-depth study of Hitler's childhood see: *For Your Own Good: Hidden Cruelty in Child-Rearing and the Roots of Violence* by Alice Miller, translated by Hildegarde and Hunter Hannum (Noonday Press, 1983).

11. *Emotional Intelligence: Why It Can Matter More Than IQ* by Daniel Goleman (Bantam Books, 1995).

12. *Toward a Psychology of Being* by Abraham H. Maslow (John Wiley & Sons, 1968).

13. *Wholeness and the Implicate Order* by David Bohm, p. 194 (ARK Paperbacks, an imprint of Routledge and Kegan Paul plc, London, 1980, 1983).

Index

The Verbally Abusive Relationship

How to Recognize It and How to Respond

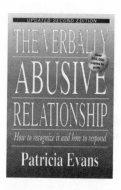

"A groundbreaking book."

—Newsweek

The Verbally Abusive Relationship helps a victim recognize manipulation and abuse at any level. It begins with a self-evaluative questionnaire and a description of the primary patterns of abuse. It then covers the categories of verbal abuse, such as accusation and trivializing, and explores the underlying dynamics of a verbally abusive relationship. This book helps the victim establish limits and boundaries, and shows how to respond effectively to verbal abuse. There are also guidelines for recovery and healing, and steps for enhancing self-esteem.

Trade paperback, 5½" x 8½", 224 pages, $14.95
ISBN: 1-55850-582-2

Verbal Abuse Survivors Speak Out

on Relationship and Recovery

Verbal Abuse Survivors Speak Out draws up on the experience of thousands who responded to Patricia Evans' first book, *The Verbally Abusive Relationship.* Their letters highlight Evans' in-depth exploration of verbal abuse issues and bring increasing clarity and insight to the reader. You will learn the stories of other women who have struggled against the fear and oppression engendered by verbal abuse, and have made the decision to insist on a change. Some of these women are just beginning to understand the problem, some are planning to leave their relationships, some have already left, and some, with their spouse, have made a commitment to change their relationship for the better. Their stories can give validation to suspicions and fears, and can provide courage, hope, and a road map for healing and recovery.

Trade paperback, 5½" x 8½", 224 pages $14.95
ISBN: 1-55850-304-8

Available wherever books are sold.
For more information, or to order, call 800-258-0929
or visit *www.adamsmedia.com*
Adams Media, 57 Littlefield Street, Avon, MA 02322